THE NIGHT PRAYERS:
QIYĀM & TARĀWĪḤ

بسم الله الرحمن الرحيم

THE NIGHT PRAYERS:
QIYĀM & TARĀWĪḤ

FROM WORKS BY

MUḤAMMAD NĀṢIR UD-DĪN AL-ALBĀNĪ

(AND OTHER SCHOLARS)

COMPILED BY

MUḤAMMAD AL-JIBĀLĪ

AL-QUR'ĀN WAS-SUNNAH SOCIETY
OF NORTH AMERICA

The Night Prayers: Qiyām and Tarāwīḥ

ISBN 1-886451-04-4

TABLE OF CONTENTS

TABLE OF CONTENTS v

PRELUDE xiii
Introduction xiii
Our *Daʿwah* and Objectives xiv
General Approach in This Work xix
Translating and Transliterating Arabic xx
Translating and Referencing *Qurʾān* and *Ḥadīth* xxii
Notable Utterances and Mnemonics xxiii
Appeal xxiv

PREFACE xxv
This Book xxv
Work Done in this Book xxvi
Acknowledgements xxviii

CHAPTER 1
INTRODUCTION 1
The *Fitnah* of Ignorance 1
Reason for Writing this Book 2
Major Topics 3
 Number of *Rakʿāt* (3)
 Other Topics (4)
A Highly Rewardable Mission 4

CHAPTER 2
QIYĀM 7
Qiyām, Tarāwīḥ, and *Witr* 7
 Definitions (7)
 Misconceptions (7)
 Tarāwīḥ (8)
The Excellence of *Qiyām* 9
 The Best Voluntary Prayer (9)

Protection from Satan's Magic (10)
Sign of Thankfulness (10)
Sign of Goodness (11)
Means of Entering *Jannah* (11)
Acceptance of Supplications (11)
Closeness to Allāh (12)
Mercy from Allāh (13)
Among the Most Righteous (13)
Constant Deeds Guarantee Ample Rewards (14)
The Excellence of *Qiyām* in *Ramaḍān* 15
Among the Most Righteous (15)
Getting Up for *Qiyām* 16
Ablution and Cleaning the Teeth (16)
Mentioning Allāh (16)
Voice Level 18

CHAPTER 3
LAYLAT UL-QADR 21
Meaning 21
Merits 21
Which Night? 23
Varying Reports and Opinions (23)
The Last Ten Nights of *Ramaḍān* (23)
The Night of the Twenty-first (24)
The Night of the Twenty-seventh (25)
Summary (25)
How to Seek *Laylat ul-Qadr* 26
Praying *Qiyām* (26)
Making Supplications (26)
Abandoning Worldly Pleasures for the Sake of Worship (27)
Signs of *Laylat ul-Qadr* 27
Authentic Signs (27)
Unfounded Folk-tales (28)

CHAPTER 4
PRAYING *TARĀWĪḤ* IN *JAMĀʿAH* 29
The Prophet's *Sunnah* 29

The Prophet's Approval (29)
The Prophet's Action (29)
The Prophet's Encouragement (34)
Reason for Discontinuing *Qiyām* in *Jamā'ah* (36)
'Umar Revives the *Sunnah* 36
'Umar's Action (36)
'Umar's Understanding (37)
Wrong Conclusions from 'Umar's Action (38)
Women Joining the *Jamā'ah* 41

CHAPTER 5
NUMBER OF *RAK'ĀT* FOR *QIYĀM* 43
Introduction 43
The Number that the Prophet Prayed 43
'Ā'ishah's Reports (43)
Jābir's Report (46)
Ibn 'Abbās's Weak Report (46)
Reports from 'Umar 49
'Umar Commands the People to Pray Eleven *Rak'āt* (49)
Weakness of the Twenty-*Rak'āt* Reports (50)
Ash-Shāfi'ī and at-Tirmiṯhī's Position (56)
Weak Reports That Do Not Reinforce Each Other (57)
Possible Reconciliation (60)
Reports from Other Companions 60
Reports from 'Alī (60)
Reports from Ubayy Bin Ka'b (62)
Report from Ibn Mas'ūd (64)
What Was the Consensus of the Companions? 65
The Maximum Permissible Number 67
The *Sunnah* of the Prophet and His Companions (67)
Is "More" Always Good? (68)
Regulated *Nafl* Prayers (70)
The Meaning of *Bid'ah* (72)
Some Scholarly Statements (73)
Clarifying Some Doubts 74
1. Difference among the Scholars (75)
2. No Text Prohibits Adding (78)

3. Reliance on General Texts (78)
4. Belittling the Great Scholars? (80)
Safety in Adhering to the *Sunnah* 82
Praying less than Eleven *Rakʿāt* 83

CHAPTER 6
MANNER OF PRAYING *QIYĀM* 85
Supplication for Starting *Qiyām* 85
1. Ibn ʿAbbās's Report (85)
2. ʿĀʾishah's Report (87)
3. Abū Saʿīd's Report (88)
Recitation During *Qiyām* 88
The Prophet's Practice (89)
ʿUmar's Practice (90)
Correct Length of Recitation (91)
Recitation in the Three *Rakʿāt* of *Witr* (91)
The Time of *Qiyām* 92
Various Ways of Performing *Qiyām* 93
Method One (93)
Method Two (96)
Method Three (96)
Method Four (98)
Method Five (98)
Method Six (99)
Other Methods (100)
The Last Three *Rakʿāt* 100
Differing from *Maghrib* (101)
Ibn Naṣr's Understanding (101)
Reconciling between Two Reports (103)
Concluding *Qiyām* 104
Qunūt (104)
What to Say at the End of *Witr* (104)
The Two *Rakʿāt* Following *Witr* (105)
Miscellaneous *Witr* Issues 106
One *Witr* per Night (106)
Missing *Witr* (107)
Praying *Witr* on Animals (108)

CHAPTER 7
QUNŪT 109
Meaning of *Qunūt* 109
Correct Reasons for *Qunūt* 110
1. Occurrence of Disasters (111)
2. Important Events that Affect the Muslims (112)
3. *Qiyām* and *Witr* (113)
Which Obligatory Prayers? 113
All Prayers (113)
A Deserted *Sunnah* (114)
During *Fajr?* (115)
Before or After *Rukū'*? 116
After *Rukū'* (116)
Before *Rukū'* (116)
The *Qunūt* of *Witr* (117)
Conclusion (118)
Miscellaneous Issues 118
Saying *Qunūt* Loudly (118)
Saying *Āmīn* (118)
Raising the Hands (118)
What to Say During the *Qunūt* of *Witr* 119
Innovations and Deviations 121
Wiping the Face (122)
Preceding *Qunūt* with *Takbīr* (122)
Extended *Qunūt* (122)
Moaning and Weeping (123)

CHAPTER 8
I'TIKĀF 125
Definition 125
Ruling 125
Weak Reports 126
Wisdom and Manners of *I'tikāf* 127
Wisdom (127)
Manners during *I'tikāf* (128)
Time of Year 128

Place for *I'tikāf* 129
A Mosque of *Jumu'ah* (129)
The Three Sacred Mosques (130)
At Home? (131)
Requirements of *I'tikāf* 131
Staying Within the *Masjid* (131)
Fasting (131)
Starting and Ending Times (132)
Minimum Stay (132)
Permitted Acts During *I'tikāf* 132
Leaving the *Masjid* for a Need (132)
Performing *Wuḍū'* Within the *Masjid* (133)
Erecting a Tent Inside the *Masjid* (133)
Using a Mattress (134)
Disapproved Acts During *I'tikāf* 134
Leaving Without Need (134)
Intercourse (134)
Worldly Involvement (135)
Women's *I'tikāf* 135

CHAPTER 9
PERFECTING THE PRAYER 139
Devotion in the Prayer 139
Reports from the Prophet and the *Salaf* (139)
Lost Devotion (140)
Glimpses of Light (141)
Ḥadīths on Perfecting the Prayer 141
Conclusion 145

CHAPTER 10
SUMMARY 147
Important Points 147
1. Praying *Tarāwīḥ* in *jamā'ah* Is a *Sunnah* (147)
2. The Correct Number in the *Sunnah* Is Eleven (147)
3. Our View of Those Who Disagree (147)
4. The *Sunnah* Is Better than the Addition (148)
5. 'Umar Revived the *Sunnah* (148)

6. The *Ṣaḥābah* Did Not Pray Twenty (148)
7. No Excuse for Adding (148)
8. Scholars Disapproving the Addition (148)
9. Position from the Great Scholars (149)
10. Lost Devotion (149)
11. Praying less than Eleven (149)
12. Various Methods for Praying *Qiyām* (149)
Lastly 149

INDEX OF ARABIC TERMS 151

PRELUDE

Introduction

Alḥamdu lillāh. Indeed, all glory and praise is due to Allāh. We glorify and praise Him and we ask Him for help and forgiveness. In Allāh we seek refuge from the evils of ourselves and from our wrong doings. He whom Allāh guides shall not be misguided, and he whom He misguides shall never be guided.

I bear witness that there is no [true] god except Allāh, alone without any partners, and I bear witness that Muḥammad (ﷺ) is His *'Abd* [1] and Messenger.

﴿يَا أَيُّهَا ٱلَّذِينَ آمَنُوا ٱتَّقُوا ٱللَّهَ حَقَّ تُقَاتِهِ وَلاَ تَمُوتُنَّ إِلاَّ وَأَنْتُم مُسْلِمُونَ۝﴾ آل عمران ١٠٢

«Believers! Fear and worship Allāh as He deserves, and do not die except as Muslims.» [2]

﴿يَا أَيُّهَا ٱلنَّاسُ ٱتَّقُوا رَبَّكُمُ ٱلَّذِي خَلَقَكُم مِنْ نَفْسٍ وَاحِدَةٍ وَخَلَقَ مِنْهَا زَوْجَهَا وَبَثَّ مِنْهُمَا رِجَالاً كَثِيرًا وَنِسَآءً وَٱتَّقُوا ٱللَّهَ ٱلَّذِي تَسَآءَلُونَ بِهِ وَٱلأَرْحَامَ إِنَّ ٱللَّهَ كَانَ عَلَيْكُمْ رَقِيبًا۝﴾ النساء ١

«People! Revere your Lord who has created you from one soul, and created from it its mate, and from these two spread forth multitudes of men and women; and fear Allāh through whom you demand [your mutual rights], and [revere the ties of] the wombs. Indeed, Allāh is ever-watchful over you.» [3]

---

1 *'Abd*: Devoted servant and worshipper.

2 *Āl 'Imrān* 3:102.

3 *An-Nisā'* 4:1.

﴿يَـٰٓأَيُّهَا ٱلَّذِينَ ءَامَنُوا۟ ٱتَّقُوا۟ ٱللَّهَ وَقُولُوا۟ قَوْلًا سَدِيدًا ۝ يُصْلِحْ لَكُمْ أَعْمَـٰلَكُمْ وَيَغْفِرْ لَكُمْ ذُنُوبَكُمْ ۗ وَمَن يُطِعِ ٱللَّهَ وَرَسُولَهُۥ فَقَدْ فَازَ فَوْزًا عَظِيمًا ۝﴾ الأحزاب ٧٠-٧١

«Believers! Revere Allāh, and [always] speak the truth. He will then direct you to do righteous deeds and will forgive your sins. And whoever obeys Allāh and His Messenger has indeed achieved a great victory.» [1]

Verily, the best words are those of Allāh (ﷻ); the best guidance is that of Muḥammad (ﷺ); the worst matters [in creed or worship] are those innovated [by people], for every such innovated matter is a *bid'ah* [2], and every *bid'ah* is an act of misguidance that deserves the Fire. [3]

Our *Da'wah* and Objectives

Our goal in this and our other works is to propagate the True *Da'wah* [4] that derives from the Book of Allāh (ﷻ) and the *Sunnah* [5] of His Messenger (ﷺ). Propagating this *Da'wah* is a duty that every Muslim should cherish. Allāh (ﷻ) says:

﴿وَلْتَكُن مِّنكُمْ أُمَّةٌ يَدْعُونَ إِلَى ٱلْخَيْرِ وَيَأْمُرُونَ بِٱلْمَعْرُوفِ وَيَنْهَوْنَ عَنِ ٱلْمُنكَرِ ۚ وَأُو۟لَـٰٓئِكَ هُمُ ٱلْمُفْلِحُونَ ۝﴾ آل عمران ١٠٤

---

1 *Al-Aḥzāb* 33:70-71.

2 *Bid'ah*: Innovation in the creed or in acts of worship.

3 These opening paragraphs are a translation of *Khuṭbat ul-Ḥājah* (the Sermon of Need) with which the Messenger (ﷺ) used to start his speeches and which he was keen to teach to his companions.

4 *Da'wah*: Call and mission.

5 *Sunnah*: Way, guidance, teachings, etc.

«Let there arise from you a group of people inviting to all that is good (*Islām*), enjoining what is right (according to *Islām*), and forbidding what is wrong (according to *Islām*). These are the ones who will achieve success.» [1]

This *Da'wah* may be summarized in two words: *tasfiyah* (cleansing and purification) and *tarbiyah* (cultivation and education). Allāh (ﷻ) refers to this in the following:

﴿هُوَ ٱلَّذِي بَعَثَ فِي ٱلْأُمِّيِّـۧنَ رَسُولًا مِّنْهُمْ يَتْلُواْ عَلَيْهِمْ ءَايَـٰتِهِۦ وَيُزَكِّيهِمْ وَيُعَلِّمُهُمُ ٱلْكِتَـٰبَ وَٱلْحِكْمَةَ وَإِن كَانُواْ مِن قَبْلُ لَفِي ضَلَـٰلٍ مُّبِينٍ۝﴾ الجمعة ٢

«He it is who has sent unto the unlettered people a Messenger from among themselves to convey unto them His messages, to purify them, and to teach them the Book and the Wisdom - whereas before that they had been, most obviously, in clear misguidance.» [2]

Propagating the True *Da'wah* must then be pursued through purifying *Islām* from baseless beliefs and practices, and working patiently to assist the Muslims abide by the true and purified religion. This must be done at various levels as follows:

1. We must uphold the sublime *Qur'ān* and the Prophet's authentic *Sunnah*, and comprehend them in accordance with the understanding and practice of the righteous *Salaf* [3]. Allāh (ﷻ) commands with this once and again. For example, He says:

---

1 *Āl 'Imrān* 3:104.

2 *Al-Jumu'ah* 62:2.

3 The *ṣaḥābah* (the Prophet's companions; singular *ṣaḥābī*) and their true followers.

﴿وَمَن يُشَاقِقِ ٱلرَّسُولَ مِنۢ بَعْدِ مَا تَبَيَّنَ لَهُ ٱلْهُدَىٰ وَيَتَّبِعْ غَيْرَ سَبِيلِ ٱلْمُؤْمِنِينَ نُوَلِّهِۦ مَا تَوَلَّىٰ وَنُصْلِهِۦ جَهَنَّمَ وَسَآءَتْ مَصِيرًا۝﴾ النساء ١١٥

«If anyone contends with the Messenger after the Guidance has been plainly conveyed to him, and follows a path other than that of the believers, We shall leave him in the path he has chosen, and land him in Hell: What an evil abode!» [1]

And He (ﷻ) says:

﴿فَإِنْ آمَنُواْ بِمِثْلِ مَآ ءَامَنتُم بِهِۦ فَقَدِ ٱهْتَدَواْ۝﴾ البقرة ١٣٧

«So if they believe as you believe [2], they are indeed on the right path.» [3]

2. We must enlighten and educate the Muslims, urging them to comply with the true *Dīn* [4], act according to its teachings, and adorn themselves with its virtues and ethics. This will ensure Allāh's acceptance, through which they will realize happiness and glory, as indicated in the following:

﴿وَٱلْعَصْرِ۝ إِنَّ ٱلإِنسَـٰنَ لَفِي خُسْرٍ۝ إِلا ٱلَّذِينَ ءَامَنُواْ وَعَمِلُواْ ٱلصَّـٰلِحَـٰتِ وَتَوَاصَوْاْ بِٱلْحَقِّ وَتَوَاصَوْاْ بِٱلصَّبْرِ۝﴾ العصر ١–٣

«By the passing time, man is indeed in loss, except those who believe, do good deeds, enjoin upon one another the keeping to truth, and enjoin upon one

1 *An-Nisā'* 4:115.

2 The address here is to the companions of the Messenger (ﷺ).

3 *Al-Baqarah* 2:137.

4 *Dīn* : Religion.

another patience in adversity.» [5]

3. We must caution Muslims and exhort them to absolve their lives of all forms of *shirk* (polytheism), *bid'ah*s, philosophy, or any other thoughts alien to the pure, essential tenets of *Islām*. This is a duty that Allāh (ﷻ) enjoins on us by saying:

﴿وَتَعَاوَنُوا۟ عَلَى ٱلْبِرِّ وَٱلتَّقْوَىٰ ۖ وَلَا تَعَاوَنُوا۟ عَلَى ٱلْإِثْمِ وَٱلْعُدْوَٰنِ﴾
المائدة ٢

«Help one another in righteousness and piety; and do not help one another in sinning and transgression.» [2]

4. We must help cleanse the *Sunnah* of weak and fabricated narrations. The weak reports and unfounded beliefs have marred the clarity of *Islām*, preventing the advancement of Muslims. This duty is of such absolute vitality that the Messenger (ﷺ) praised those who perform it by saying:

‹This knowledge will be carried by the trustworthy ones of every generation - they will expel from it the alterations made by those going beyond bounds, the false claims of the liars, and the false interpretations of the ignorant.› [3]

5. We must strive to revive unobstructed *Islām*ic thought within the boundaries of *Islām*ic principles [4], oppose stubborn adherence to *mathhab*s [5], and oppose prejudiced loyalty to parties. Neglecting

---

1 *Al-'Aṣr* 103:1-3.

2 *Al-Mā'idah* 5:2.

3 Authentic - Reported by Ibn *'Adiyy and others.*

4 These principles are described in point "1" above.

5 *Mathhab*: Way or approach. It mostly refers to one of the four *Islām*ic schools of legislation and jurisprudence that were based on the research and understanding of

this in the past has caused rust to dwell on the hearts and minds of Muslims, diverting them from the pure original sources of *Islām*, and causing them to deviate from the honest *Islām*ic brotherhood called to by Allāh (ﷻ):

﴿وَٱعْتَصِمُواْ بِحَبْلِ ٱللَّهِ جَمِيعًا وَلَا تَفَرَّقُواْ۝﴾ آل عمران ١٠٣

«And hold fast all together, by the rope of Allāh, and be not divided among yourselves.» [1]

And by His Messenger (ﷺ):

‹Be, worshippers of Allāh, one brethren.› [2]

6. We must help provide realistic *Islām*ic solutions to contemporary problems, and strive to resume a true *Islām*ic way of life and establish a true *Islām*ic society governed by Allāh's law. Allāh (ﷻ) says:

﴿وَأَنِ ٱحْكُم بَيْنَهُم بِمَا أَنزَلَ ٱللَّهُ وَلَا تَتَّبِعْ أَهْوَاءَهُمْ﴾ المائدة ٤٩

«Hence, judge between them in accordance with what Allāh has revealed, and do not follow their errant views.» [3]

We call upon all Muslims to support us in carrying out this noble trust. This will surely elevate and honor them and spread the eternal message of *Islām* all over the Earth, as is Allāh's true promise:

﴿هُوَ ٱلَّذِي أَرْسَلَ رَسُولَهُ بِٱلْهُدَىٰ وَدِينِ ٱلْحَقِّ لِيُظْهِرَهُ عَلَى ٱلدِّينِ

---

the Four *Imāms* (scholars): Abū Ḥanīfah an-Nuʿmān Bin Thābit, Mālik Bin Anas, Aḥmad Bin Ḥanbal, and Muḥammad Bin Idrīs ash-Shāfiʿī - May Allāh (ﷻ) bestow His mercy on them all.

1 *Āl ʿImrān* 3:103.

2 Al-Bukhārī and Muslim.

3 *Al-Māʾidah* 5:49.

كُلِّهِ وَلَوْ كَرِهَ ٱلْمُشْرِكُونَ۝﴾ الصف ٩

«He it is who has sent His Messenger with Guidance and the Religion of Truth, in order to make it prevail over all [false] religion, however hateful this may be to the *mushriks* (those who ascribe divinity to other than Allāh).» [1]

General Approach in This Work

A large number of *Islām*ic writings in recent times lack the correctness and preciseness of a true *Islām*ic approach. They suffer from two major problems:

1. Unconcern about the importance of relying only on authentic evidence, particularly in quoting *Ḥadīth* [2]. Thus some conclusions that they reach, and some principles that they establish, are, in the least, of doubtful validity.

2. Replacing the glorious thought and sound understanding of the early righteous pioneers and scholars of *Islām* (the *Salaf* ﷺ) by inferior opinions and speculations of later scholars.

These problems led to the following serious consequences:

- A deformation in some of the fundamental beliefs for the majority of Muslims, including many who are regarded as scholars.
- Practicing *Islām* in a way that conflicts with the teachings of Muḥammad (ﷺ).

---

1 *Aṣ-Ṣaff* 61:9.

2 *Ḥadīth*: Reports of the Prophet's sayings, actions, and approvals. Our convention is to use *ḥadīth* (plural *ḥadīths*) with lower case ḥ to indicate single report(s), and *Ḥadīth* with upper case Ḥ to indicate the subject of *Ḥadīth* specialty.

Through the ages, only few true scholars (*'ulamā'*) have directed their efforts to correcting these problems through reviving the authentic *Sunnah* and fighting *bid'ahs*. Their efforts have always been greatly countered and fiercely rejected by their contemporaries. But there is no way to stop truth from spreading, and Allāh's Light will surely be complete and prevalent. These *'ulamā'* (may Allāh bless them and reward their efforts) have produced marvelous writings that have rectified the *Islām*ic beliefs and practices.

Very little of these great writings have been translated to English, or have been resorted to in English writings on *Islām*. Thus a good deal of the existing *Islām*ic literature in English suffers from the two problems cited earlier. It also suffers from additional problems, mainly:

3. Many writers have had a shallow *Islām*ic education. They had to self-educate themselves to meet the requirements of *da'wah* in the West. But their education has not been, in general, adequate enough to qualify them to write on *Islām*.

4. Some non-Muslim scholars and orientalists have volunteered to write on *Islām*. Despite their wide academic knowledge, their writings on *Islām* are usually charged with obvious fallacies and prejudiced misinformation.

These problems have caused a further deviation from the truth in many of today's English writings and talks on *Islām*.

This publication is, therefore, a humble response to our realization of a great responsibility: the responsibility to help bring forth, before the general English speaking public, writings that refine the *Islām*ic concepts from the above problems and present *Islām* pure and simple, as close as possible to the way that it was understood and practiced by its early good pioneers - the *Salaf*.

Translating and Transliterating Arabic

Attempt has been made to minimize the use of Arabic terms. This is a frequently neglected service to the English speaking reader.

Transliterated Arabic terms are used in the following two situations only:

a) When no English expression is found that can reflect the same meaning as the original term.

b) When it is judged that an Arabic term is of such importance that it is essential to familiarize the readers with it.

In such cases, the Arabic terms are defined at their first occurrence, between brackets or in a footnote. They are then include in the INDEX OF ARABIC TERMS, usually appearing at the end of the book.

Except for proper nouns, transliterated Arabic terms are *italic*ized. In general, the rules of English pronunciation can be applied. The following table includes additional symbols employed in this book to help pronounce the Arabic terms.

Symbol	Stands for	English Equivalent Sounds
ā, Ā	*Alif* (long vowel a)	Mostly: M<u>a</u>n, s<u>a</u>d. At times: F<u>a</u>ther, h<u>a</u>rd, g<u>o</u>d.
ū, Ū	*Wāw* (long vowel u)	R<u>oo</u>t, s<u>ou</u>p, fl<u>u</u>te.
ī, Ī	*Yā'* (long vowel i)	S<u>ee</u>d, l<u>ea</u>n, p<u>ie</u>ce, rec<u>ei</u>ve.
'	*Hamzah*	The first consonant vocal sound uttered when saying: <u>a</u>t, <u>i</u>t or <u>o</u>h.
Th, th	*Thā'*	<u>Th</u>ree, mo<u>th</u>.
Ḥ, ḥ	*Ḥā'*	No equivalent. Produced in the lower throat, below "h". Resembles the sound produced after swallowing.

Symbol	Stands for	English Equivalent Sounds
Kh, kh	*Khā'*	No equivalent. Produced in the back of the mouth and top of the throat.
Th, th	*Thāl*	There, mother.
Ṣ, ṣ	*Ṣād*	A deeper "s" sound. Somewhat close to the "sc" in "muscle".
Ḍ, ḍ	*Ḍād*	Sounds deeper than a "d". Produced by touching the tongue to the mouth's roof.
Ṭ, ṭ	*Ṭah*	Similar but deeper than a "t".
Ẓ, ẓ	*Ẓah*	A deeper *thāl*, produced by touching the tip of the tongue to the back of the front teeth.
ʿ	*ʿAyn*	Produced in the bottom of the throat, underneath "ḥ".
Gh, gh	*Ghayn*	A gurgling sound produced in the back of the mouth, just above the *khā'*. Similar to the "R" in some french accents.
Q, q	*Qāf*	Somewhat similar to the "c" in "coffee".

Translating and Referencing *Qur'ān* and *Ḥadīth*

The *Qur'ān* contains Allāh's exact words. These words cannot be exactly translated into other languages because of possible misinterpretations and limited human understanding. It is best to translate the meanings as understood by the Muslim scholars. This is what is attempted here. When an *āyah* [1] is cited, the Arabic text is quoted first, followed, between double angle quotation marks («»), by the English meaning in **boldface**. The meaning is extracted from books of *tafsīr* (*Qur'ān*ic commentaries and interpretations) and from accessible translations.

The location of a *Qur'ān*ic citation is specified in a footnote. It provides the name of the *sūrah* (*Qur'ān*ic chapter) followed by its number and the number(s) of the *āyah*(s) cited.

In general, the Arabic text of a cited *ḥadīth* is not provided. This is based on a general agreement among the *'ulamā'* permitting relating *ḥadīth*s by meaning. The meaning of a *ḥadīth* is included, in **boldface**, between single angle quotation marks (‹›).

A footnote normally specifies the location of a cited *ḥadīth* in the *Ḥadīth* compilations. The footnote indicates as well its degree of authenticity and the names of scholars who made such judgement. If a *ḥadīth* is narrated by al-Bukhārī or Muslim, its authenticity is taken for granted.

Notable Utterances and Mnemonics

Out of love, appreciation, gratitude or other related noble feelings, a Muslim is encouraged to utter certain phrases at the mention of Allāh, His messengers, the *ṣaḥābah*, or other righteous Muslims. For printing and space reasons, instead of presenting the complete phrase, a condensed Arabic statement is provided in some cases, and a mnemonic is employed in others, as follows:

(﷾) *Subḥānahū wa ta'ālā*: a phrase uttered at the mention of Allāh, meaning, "He is exalted above all weakness or indignity".

(ﷺ) *Ṣalla 'Llāhu 'alayhi wa sallam* [2]: a phrase uttered at the

1 *Āyah*: A *Qur'ān*ic phrase approximately equal to one sentence, but sometimes longer or shorter than that. Its plural is *āyāt*.

2 Uttering this is sometimes described as, "saying *ṣalāh* upon the messenger(s)".

mention of Muḥammad or other messengers, meaning, "May Allāh's peace and praise be on him".

(﵁) *Raḍiya 'Llāhu ʿanhu*: a phrase uttered at the mention of one of the male *ṣaḥābah* meaning, "May Allāh be pleased with him".

(﵃) *Raḍiya 'Llāhu ʿanhum*: a phrase uttered at the mention of three or more of the male *ṣaḥābah* meaning, "May Allāh be pleased with them".

(R) *Raḍiya 'Llāhu ʿanhā*: a mnemonic of "May Allāh be pleased with her" or the plural thereof. This is uttered at the mention of one or more of the female *ṣaḥābah*.

(r) *Raḥimahu 'Llāh*: a mnemonic of "May Allāh have mercy on him" or the feminine or plural thereof. It is said at the mention of past *ʿulamā'* and pious Muslims other than the *ṣaḥābah*.

When coming across any of these symbols, the reader is advised to utter the complete phrase in order to obtain the reward of saying the appropriate thikr (remembrance) or *duʿā'* (invocation).

Appeal

In this work, great care has been taken to present *Islām* in a pure and accurate manner. Yet, no human work can be devoid of mistakes. We appeal to the readers who encounter mistakes to kindly write and point them out to us, and to ask Allāh (ﷻ) to forgive us.

The Publisher

PREFACE

With Allāh's (ﷻ) blessing and bounty, our practice has been to present to the readers materials that clarify the *Sunnah* in the most authentic and simple way. In line with this, we tackle in this book a subject that is largely misunderstood, though much needed by the Muslims, both in *Ramaḍān* and around the year: that of the voluntary night prayers.

This Book

This book is, for the most part, a precise translation of two works by the *ʿallāmah* (great scholar) Muḥammad Nāṣir ud-Dīn al-Albānī, namely, *Ṣalāt ut-Tarāwīḥ* and *Qiyāmu Ramaḍān*.

Al-Albānī states in his introduction to the latter book that it is mostly a summary of the earlier:

> "Our book *Ṣalāt ut-Tarāwīḥ* was printed quite a while ago, and the need has now arisen to reprint it. In terms of the style in which it was written, that book has fulfilled its goals – most importantly, alerting the common people to the correct *sunnah* regarding the *tarāwīḥ* prayer, and refuting those who rejected it. By that, this *sunnah* spread in many *masjid*s (mosques) in Syria, Jordan, and other Muslim countries – all praise is due to Allāh (ﷻ), with Whose blessing all good deeds are accomplished. Thus, I decided to abridge that book in a purely scholarly style, without including any of the refutations, in accordance with the saying, 'Say your peace and go.' I summarized all of the scholarly concepts in the original book, and added others to them for additional benefit. It is Allāh (ﷻ) that we ask to benefit people with it, as he did with the previous one, and to reward me for it, He is the most generous one to ask."

However, there are many important discussions and concepts present in the earlier book but omitted in the later. Thus, it was considered very important to present the English reader with a combined book, preserving the discussions from both works, and omitting – as much as possible – discussions which are redundant between them, or, in some cases, even in various places of the earlier work.

Thus, this work presents an accurate account of al-Albānī's discussions in both of his books, preserving most of his original words, and rearranging that for a better flow of ideas.

Furthermore, al-Albānī's work was supplemented with additional material by various authors, especially in sections or chapters where his discussion was very brief and incomplete.

Work Done in this Book

From the above, it is clear that this book has two main goals:

a. Providing a complete manual on the subject of *qiyām* and related issues.

b. Presenting the English reader with two important works by the great scholar al-Albānī.

In order to fulfill both goals, and at the same time keep the book in a presentable and easy to understand format for the readers, the following steps were applied:

1. Both works by al-Albānī were completely translated. This was especially pain-staking in the case of the earlier work, because of its numerous extensive and specialized discussions of *Ḥādīth* issues.

2. Sections that were meant as personal refutations of a specific person or group of people were omitted.

3. Both books were combined.

4. The material was reorganized so as to make it flow in a logical manner. In the process, numerous new headings and subheadings were introduced to help the readers quickly find any specific topic of interest.

5. Redundant concepts, discussions, or reports were omitted – except in some cases, where the repetition was considered warranted. In many cases, cross referencing was applied to reports appearing in various parts of this book.

6. Analysis of the authenticity of narrations was moved from the main text to footnotes. This was not always possible, as some of the sections only deal with such analysis. On the other hand, all other explanatory remarks were moved from the footnotes to the main text.

7. Footnotes and commentaries were added to explain specialized terms from *ʿIlm ul-Ḥādīth* or other *Islām*ic terms and concepts.

8. Materials from other sources were added to supplement the material in those two works. However, to keep al-Albānī's work distinctive, alerting footnotes are placed next to the titles of chapters or sections where major portions are added – namely, Chapters 2, 3, 7, and 8, and the first and last sections of Chapter 6. The main sources consulted for the additional material are:

   Aḥkām ul-Qunūt by ʿAdnān ʿArʿūr.
   Al-Inṣāf fī Aḥkām il-Iʿtikāf by ʿAlī al-Ḥalabī.
   Al-Jāmiʿu li Aḥkām il-Qurʾān by al-Qurṭubī.
   Bughyat ul-Insān fī Waẓāʾifi Ramaḍān by Ibn Rajab al-Ḥanbalī.
   Fatḥ ul-Bārī by al-Ḥāfiẓ Ibn Ḥajar.
   Irshād us-Sārī (v. 3) by Muḥammad Ibrāhīm Shaqrah.
   Irwāʾ ul-Ghalīl by al-Albānī.
   Lisān ul-ʿArab by Ibn Manẓūr.
   Mishkāt ul-Maṣābīḥ by al-Khaṭāb ut-Tabrīzī / al-Albānī.

Ṣifatu Ṣawm in-Nabī by Salīm al-Hilālī and ʿAlī al-Ḥalabī.
Zād ul-Maʿād by Ibn ul-Qayyim.

Acknowledgements

All praise and thanks are offered to our Lord (ﷻ) for facilitating the completion of this work. Deep appreciation and gratitude is due to the large number of Muslims who helped and supported this effort in various ways - may Allāh (ﷻ) reward them all. In particular, I would like to express appreciation of the great help provided by two persons:

a) Abū Khalīl al-Amrīkī, who helped translate a good portion of the later book of al-Albānī, patiently reviewed the manuscript of this work, and provided important suggestions.

b) ʿAbdullāh al-Jibālī, who helped with the book's layout, typed all the Arabic text, and designed the cover.

I ask Allāh (ﷻ) to make this humble effort helpful and fruitful to the Muslims, forgive our shortcomings, purify our work from hypocrisy and conceit, and accept it from us.

Our Lord, forgive us and all of the believers, and bestow Your peace and praise upon our Prophet Muḥammad (ﷺ).

Muhammad al-Jibaly
10 *Rajab* 1417 H
21 November 1996

CHAPTER 1

INTRODUCTION

The *Fitnah* of Ignorance

Indeed, Ibn Masʿūd was truthful when he said:

> **"What will you do when a *fitnah* (mishap; deviation) prevails over you, causing an adult person to turn old, and a child to turn into an adult? People will adopt it as *sunnah*; and if one neglected any part of it, he will be told, 'You neglected the *Sunnah!*'"**

He (ﷺ) was asked, "When will this happen?" And he replied:

> **"It will happen when your *ʿulamāʾ* are gone; you will have many reciters, but few *fuqahāʾ* (people with true understanding of *Islām*); you will have many leaders, but few trusted ones; worldly gains will be sought with deeds of the hereafter; and people will seek the knowledge, but not for the sake of *Dīn*."** [1]

This report, *mawqūf* [2] though it is, takes the status of *marfūʿ* [3] because it mentions matters of *ghayb* [4] that cannot be known except through revelation.

---

1 Recorded by ad-Dārimī with two *isnāds*, one of which is *ṣaḥīḥ* (authentic) and the other *ḥasan* (good, but not as strong as a *ṣaḥīḥ* report). It is also recorded by al-Ḥākim and Ibn ʿAbd il-Barr in *Jāmiʿu Bayān il-ʿIlm.*

2 A report "stopping" at a *ṣaḥābī*, and appearing to be his own words or opinion, without being raised to the Prophet (ﷺ).

3 A report "raised" up to the Prophet (ﷺ).

4 Matters beyond human perception.

In this *ḥadīth*, we can see signs of Muḥammad's (ﷺ) prophethood and the truthfulness of his message. *Bidʿah*s are rampant, and most Muslims are fervent in following them and calling others to them. Those most keen to adhere to the *Sunnah* and fight *bidʿah*s are labelled as followers of *bidʿah*s and neglectors of *Sunnah*! Their sole crime is that they reject innovations and refuse to participate in deviation!

This is what happened to us, followers of the *Sunnah*, in many countries and lands. We revived the *sunnah* of praying eleven *rakʿāt* for *tarāwīḥ* [1], maintaining, as much as possible, outward serenity and submission, and uttering correct authentic *thikr* (remembrance of Allāh) – all of which being neglected by most people who pray twenty *rakʿāt*.

This caused a great disturbance and fury among those who have been brought up and nurtured upon *taqlīd* (blind imitation). They attacked us severely in their talks, sermons, and books – all of which were usually void of useful knowledge and reliable evidence, and full of curses and profanities. Such is the habit of the people of falsehood when they rise against the people of truth.

This will not stop or deter us from pursuing our noble mission of spreading the *Sunnah* far and wide, in all aspects of *Islām*, *in shāʾa 'Llāh*.

Reason for Writing This Book

Many authors have written books claiming that praying twenty *rakʿāt* for *tarāwīḥ* is an established *sunnah* among the Muslims, and that, with the exception of Abū Bakr aṣ-Ṣiddīq (ﷺ), all of the Rightly Guided *Khulafāʾ* (Prophet's Successors) were consistent in praying that number. They further attribute innovation in the *Dīn* to ʿUmar (ﷺ), because he gathered the people for *tarāwīḥ* in *jamāʿah*.

Therefore, we set out to prove that ʿUmar did not innovate in this prayer – neither in number nor in gathering people for it. Rather, he was the best example of a believer who adhered closely to the *Sunnah* of his Prophet (ﷺ). It is incumbent that we clarify this truth to the

1 *Rakʿāt*: Prayer units; singular *rakʿah*. It derives from the verb *rakaʿa* which means "bowed down". The reason for this name is that each prayer unit contains one *rukūʿ* (bowing).

people, so that they would not be misguided by false claims against the Prophet (ﷺ), the Commander of the Believers ʿUmar (رضي الله عنه), or others among our righteous *Salaf*.

Major Topics

The discussion in this book centers around the *qiyām* prayer in general, and the number of its *rakʿāt* in particular.

Number of *Rakʿāt*

In terms of the number of *rakʿāt* for *qiyām*, we will establish the following:

1. The Prophet (ﷺ) did not pray more than eleven *rakʿāt* for *qiyām* (thirteen if we count the two short introductory *rakʿāt*).

2. ʿUmar (رضي الله عنه) commanded Ubayy Bin Kaʿb (رضي الله عنه) and Tamīm ad-Dārī (رضي الله عنه) to lead the people in *tarāwīḥ* with eleven *rakʿāt*, in accordance with the authentic *Sunnah*.

3. All reports that the people at the time of ʿUmar (رضي الله عنه), or any of the noble *ṣaḥābah*, prayed twenty *rakʿāt* are unauthentic and contradict the truly established reports. Similarly, all claims that the *ṣaḥābah* (رضي الله عنهم) have made an *ijmāʿ* (consensus) to pray twenty *rakʿāt* are baseless.

4. Even if a weak report were considered authentic by some people, one should still follow the well established authentic report, because it agrees with the number established in the *Sunnah*. One may not desert the *Sunnah* for anybody's understanding or practice.

5. With our certitude that the Prophet's (ﷺ) consistent practice is the best, it becomes obvious that one should adhere to the number established in the *Sunnah*, and refrain from adding to it. This has been the position of many *ʿulamāʾ*.

6. And even if we concede to the often misquoted and misunderstood statement that, "There are good innovations," we must adhere to the consensus among the scholars that following *Sunnah* is better than any innovation. ʿAbdullāh Bin Masʿūd (ﷺ) said:

> "Doing little according to the *Sunnah* is better than doing much in way of *bidʿah*." [1]

Other Topics

We will also establish in this book that the Prophet's (ﷺ) *Sunnah* is to pray *tarāwīḥ* in *jamāʿah*, to pray it as eleven *rakʿāt*, and that the *ṣaḥābah* revived and followed the *Sunnah* in that.

Furthermore, we present the different manners in which the Prophet (ﷺ) prayed *witr*, the importance of devotion in the prayer, and many other useful hints and reminders throughout the book.

We ask Allāh (ﷻ) to guide us to the truth in what we have written here and elsewhere, to make this work pure and sincere for His glorious Face, and cause our believing brethren to benefit from it – indeed He is the most Generous and Merciful.

A Highly Rewardable Mission

We establish the above with clear proofs from the authentic *Sunnah* and trustworthy narrations. By this, we hope to deliver the teachings of the *Sunnah* to people, whether in regard to this or other issues, fulfilling by that the Prophet's (ﷺ) command:

> **‹Convey (the knowledge) from me – even one *āyah*, ...›** [2]

For those who are convinced by this, and adhere to it, they would

---

1 This is an authentic report recorded by ad-Dārimī, al-Bayhaqī, and al-Ḥākim. The latter verified it to be authentic – to which ath-Thahabī agreed.

2 Al-Bukhārī and Muslim.

be successful and happy in both lives; and we would receive a multiple reward, *in shā'a 'Llāh*, because the Prophet (ﷺ) said:

> **‹Whoever starts a good way in *Islām*, he gets a reward for this, and a reward equal to that of each one who follows him into it – until the day of judgement – without reducing any of their rewards.›** [1]

For those who are not convinced, because of some doubts that they could not clarify, then there is no blame on them, because what applies to them applies equally to many great scholars in regard to this issue.

As for those who reject it based on their *hawā* (desires), or passion to adhere to the way of their parents and grandparents, Allāh (ﷻ) is their judge.

In all cases, we seek by this Allāh's (ﷻ) help, facilitation, and acceptance – He is All Hearing and Answering.

---

1 Muslim and others.

CHAPTER 2

QIYĀM [1]

Qiyām, Tarāwīḥ, and *Witr*

DEFINITIONS

Qiyām means "standing"; and *qiyām ul-layl* means "standing at night". In the *sharʿ* (*Islām*ic legislation) context, both terms refer to the same thing, namely, "The voluntary night prayer, whose time extends from after *ʿishāʾ* prayer [2] until dawn." It is described with this term (standing), because it involves long standing in which long portions of *Qurʾān* are recited.

Other common names for it are: *ṣalāt ul-layl* (the night prayer), *tahajjud* (from *hajada*: remained awake at night), *witr* (odd-numbered), and *tarāwīḥ* (resting). [3]

Witr in particular has two different meanings in the *Sunnah*, and both will be used in this book. It usually refers to the last one or three *rakʿāt* of *qiyām*. But it sometimes means all of the night prayer because, altogether, it is odd numbered.

MISCONCEPTIONS

Some people think that *tahajjud* is a night prayer different from *qiyām* or *tarāwīḥ*. Others think that *nafl* (voluntary; supererogatory) prayers at night are only recommended during *Ramaḍān*.

Thus it is important to clarify these misunderstandings, and to

---

1 For the most part, this chapter is not from the work translated from al-Albānī, but was included here for the sake of completeness. The references used for this material are mentioned in the Preface.

2 The last of the five obligatory prayers. Its time extends from the disappearance of the reddish light in the sky until the middle of the night.

3 Definitions from: *Lisān ul-ʿArab* under "*Hajada*" and "*Rawaḥa*".

emphasize what was mentioned above, i.e., that there is only one *nafl* prayer at night, with different names used to describe it. Even though *tarāwīḥ* is most commonly used to describe it in *Ramaḍān*, this does not make it a different prayer.

Furthermore, in some counties and *masjids*, mostly during the second half of *Ramaḍān*, people pray *tarāwīḥ* early in the night, and then pray another prayer that they call *tahajjud* at the end of night. This practice is a *bidʿah* because it has no basis in the *Sunnah*.

TARĀWĪḤ

From the earliest times, the Muslims have used the name *tarāwīḥ* to describe the night prayer of *Ramaḍān*. Most scholars allow using this name; but some have reservations because it carries the implication that one must rest after every four *rakʿāt* of *tarāwīḥ* – a thing that has no basis in the *Sunnah*. According to Muḥammad Shaqrah:

> "The reason for this name is that, due to long recitation, the people used to rest after every four *rakʿāt*. This rest became a necessary element of *tarāwīḥ*, even with very short recitations. This led people to think that this is a correct name revealed to Allāh's Messenger (ﷺ).
>
> It is important to clarify that this name is wrong both in text and meaning. As for text, it is not known that the Prophet (ﷺ) gave it this name, nor any of his companions ... And as for meaning, it is not known that the Prophet (ﷺ) taught his companions to rest after every four *rakʿāt*.
>
> Thus, it should be brought to the attention of people that this is a novel name. It is better to use the name that the Prophet (ﷺ) used for this prayer: *qiyām* ...
>
> One might ask, 'Is it wrong to rest after finishing two or four *rakʿāt*?' My answer is, 'If the *imām* (leader) gets tired, or feels that the people praying behind him are tired from long standing and recitation,

he may allow some rest ...' " [1]

The Excellence of *Qiyām*

There are many *āyāt* proclaiming the excellence of *qiyām* and the merit of those who perform it on a regular basis. For example, Allāh (ﷻ) describes the believers who deserve *Jannah* (paradise) as follows:

﴿تَتَجَافَىٰ جُنُوبُهُمْ عَنِ ٱلْمَضَاجِعِ يَدْعُونَ رَبَّهُمْ خَوْفًا وَطَمَعًا وَمِمَّا رَزَقْنَـٰهُمْ يُنفِقُونَ۝﴾ السجدة ١٦

«Their (the believers') sides forsake their beds, to invoke their Lord in fear and hope; and they spend out of what We bestowed on them.» [2]

﴿كَانُوا قَلِيلاً مِّنَ ٱلَّيْلِ مَا يَهْجَعُونَ۝﴾ الذاريات ١٧

«They (the pious ones) used to sleep but little at night .» [3]

In addition, there are numerous *ḥadīth*s on this subject. In what follows we present a selection of the most common ones.

THE BEST VOLUNTARY PRAYER

Abū Hurayrah (ﷺ) reported that the Prophet (ﷺ) said:

‹The best of prayers, after those prescribed, is that in the depth of night.› [4]

ʿAbdullāh Bin ʿAmr (ﷺ) reported that Allāh's Messenger (ﷺ)

1 *Irshād us-Sārī* (p. 75-77).

2 *As-Sajdah* 32:16.

3 *Ath-Thāriyāt* 51:17.

4 Muslim and Aḥmad.

said:

> **‹The most beloved prayer to Allāh was Dāwūd's. He slept one half of the night, got up (and prayed) for one third, and then slept (the remaining) one sixth.›** [1]

Protection from Satan's Magic

Abū Hurayrah (ﷺ) reported that the Prophet (ﷺ) said:

> **‹When one of you goes to sleep, Satan ties three knots over the rear of his head, blowing into each knot, "You have a long night, so sleep on." If one wakes up and mentions Allāh, one knot loosens. If he makes *wuḍū'* (ablution for prayer), another knot loosens. And if he prays, the third knot loosens, so that he becomes lively and good-natured; otherwise, he gets up ill-natured and lazy.›** [2]

Sign of Thankfulness

Al-Mughīrah (ﷺ) reported that Allāh's Messenger (ﷺ) used to stand in prayer for so long that his feet swelled. He was asked, "Why should you do this, O Allāh's Messenger, when all of your sins, past and future, have been forgiven?" He replied:

> **‹Shouldn't I be a thankful servant?›** [3]

He (ﷺ) gave this answer to 'Ā'ishah (R) as well, when she saw that his long standing in prayer caused his feet cracked, and she asked him, "Why should you do this, O Allāh's Messenger, when all of your sins, past and future, have been forgiven?" [4]

---

1 Al-Bukhārī and Muslim.

2 Al-Bukhārī and Muslim.

3 Al-Bukhārī and Muslim.

4 Al-Bukhārī and Muslim.

Sign of Goodness

ʿAbdullāh Bin ʿUmar (رضي الله عنه) reported that Allāh's Messenger (ﷺ) said:

> **‹ʿAbdullāh (Bin ʿUmar) would indeed be a good man if he prayed at night.›**

ʿAbdullāh's son, Sālim, reported that after the Prophet (ﷺ) said this, his father would not sleep at night but very little.[1]

Means of Entering *Jannah*

ʿAbdullāh Bin Salām (رضي الله عنه) reported that the Prophet (ﷺ) said:

> **‹O people! Spread (the greeting of) *salām*, provide food (to the needy), and pray at night while the people are asleep – you would then enter *Jannah* with peace.›**[2]

Acceptance of Supplications

Abū Hurayrah (رضي الله عنه) reported that the Prophet (ﷺ) said:

> **‹Our Lord (تبارك وتعالى) descends every night to the lowest heaven, when only one third of the night has remained. He says, "Who would invoke Me, so that I would answer him? Who would ask Me, so that I would give him? Who would seek My forgiveness, so that I would forgive him.›**[3]

In one of the reports, he adds:

> **‹Then Allāh extends His hand and says, "Who wants**

1 Al-Bukhārī and Muslim.

2 Recorded by at-Tirmi<u>th</u>ī. Verified to be authentic by al-Albānī.

3 Al-Bukhārī and Muslim.

to invest (good deeds) with the One who is not wasteful or unjust?" He continues to say this until the dawn arrives.› ¹

Jābir (☞) reported that he heard the Prophet (☞) say:

‹There is an hour of the night which, no Muslim person encounters it and asks for a good thing in this life or the hereafter, but Allāh grants it to him. This happens every night.› ²

Abū Umāmah (☞) reported that the Prophet (☞) was asked, "When are supplications most acceptable?" He replied:

‹In the last depth of night, and at the end of the prescribed prayers.› ³

Mu'ā<u>th</u> Bin Jabal (☞) reported that Allāh's Messenger (☞) said:

‹Whenever a Muslim goes to bed in a pure state (with *wuḍū*'), falls asleep while mentioning Allāh, and then wakes up during the night, and asks Allāh for anything good, He grants it to him.› ⁴

CLOSENESS TO ALLĀH

'Amr Bin 'Abasah (☞) reported that Allāh's Messenger (☞) said:

‹The closest that a servant is to his Lord is in the last part of night. If you can be among those who remember Allāh at that hour, do so.› ⁵

---

1 Muslim.
2 Muslim.
3 Recorded by at-Tirmi<u>th</u>ī. It is *ḥasan* according to him as well as al-Albānī.
4 Recorded by Aḥmad and Abū Dāwūd; verified to be authentic by al-Albānī.
5 Recorded by at-Tirmi<u>th</u>ī. It is authentic according to al-Ḥākim, a<u>th</u>-<u>Th</u>ahabī, and al-

MERCY FROM ALLĀH

Abū Hurayrah (﷜) reported that the Prophet (ﷺ) said:

‹May Allāh have mercy on a man who wakes up at night, prays, and wakes his wife to pray; and if she refuses, he sprinkles water on her face. And may Allāh have mercy on a woman who wakes up at night, prays, and wakes her husband to pray; and if he refuses, she sprinkles water on his face.› [1]

AMONG THE MOST RIGHTEOUS

Abū Saʿīd al-Khudrī (﷜) and Hurayrah (﷜) reported that the Prophet (ﷺ) said:

‹When a man wakes his wife at night, and they pray two rakʿāt together, they are recorded among the men and women who remember Allāh frequently.› [2]

ʿAbdullāh Bin ʿAmr (﷜) reported that the Prophet (ﷺ) said:

‹Whoever prays qiyām reciting ten āyāt, he will not be recorded among the negligent. Whoever prays qiyām reciting one hundred āyāt, he will be recorded among the devout. And whoever prays qiyām reciting one thousand āyāt, he will be recorded among those with a multitude of good deeds.› [3]

Albānī.

[1] Recorded by Abū Dāwūd and an-Nasāʾī. It is authentic according to al-Ḥākim, ath-Thahabī, and an-Nawawī. Al-Albānī said that its isnād is ḥasan.

[2] Recorded by Abū Dāwūd and Ibn Mājah; it is authentic according to al-Ḥākim, ath-Thahabī, al-ʿIrāqī, an-Nawawī, and al-Albānī.

[3] Recorded by Abū Dāwūd. Al-Albānī verified it to be ḥasan.

Constant Deeds Guarantee Ample Rewards

'Ā'ishah (R) reported that the Prophet (ﷺ) said:

> **‹The most beloved deeds to Allāh are the most constant, even if they were little.›** [1]

Also, Masrūq reported that he asked 'Ā'ishah (R), "Which deeds were most beloved to Allāh's Messenger (ﷺ)?" She replied, "The constant ones." He asked, "And when did he get up (to pray) at night." She replied, "He used to get up when he heard the rooster's crow." [2]

'Abdullāh Bin 'Amr reported that the Prophet (ﷺ) said to him:

> **‹O 'Abdallāh, do not be like such and such. He used to get up to pray at night, then he stopped doing it.›**[3]

'Ā'ishah (R) said:

> "Do not ever stop praying *qiyām*. The Prophet (ﷺ) never ceased praying it. When he was sick or weak, he prayed sitting." [4]

And she said:

> "When the Prophet (ﷺ) grew old and weak, he mostly prayed (at night) while sitting." [5]

---

1 Al-Bukhārī and Muslim.

2 Al-Bukhārī and Muslim.

3 Al-Bukhārī and Muslim.

4 Recorded by Abū Dāwūd; it is authentic according to al-Albānī.

5 Al-Bukhārī and Muslim.

The Excellence of *Qiyām* in *Ramaḍān*

There are many *ḥadīth*s describing the excellence of *qiyām* particularly in the nights of *Ramaḍān*. In the following we present a few of them.

FORGIVENESS OF SINS

Abū Hurayrah (⌘) reported:

> "Allāh's Messenger (⌘) encouraged the people, without making it an absolute command, to perform *qiyām* during *Ramaḍān*. He used to say:
>
> ‹Whoever stands (in *qiyām*) in *Ramaḍān* out of faith and expectation (of Allāh's reward), all his previous sins will be forgiven.›
>
> This continued until Allāh's Messenger (⌘) passed, and then during the *khilāfah* [1] of Abū Bakr (⌘) and a portion of that of 'Umar (⌘)." [2]

AMONG THE MOST RIGHTEOUS

'Amr Bin Murrah al-Juhanī said:

> "A man from the tribe of Quḍā'ah asked the Messenger (⌘), 'O Allāh's Messenger, what if I testified that there is no (true) god except Allāh and that you are Allāh's Messenger, prayed the five prayers, fasted the Month, stood for *qiyām* in *Ramaḍān*, and paid the *zakāh* (obligatory alms)?' The Prophet (⌘) replied:
>
> ‹Anyone dying like this will be among the *ṣiddīqīn*

---

1   *Khilāfah*: Period of rule of a *khalīfah* (successor), who succeeds the Prophet (⌘) in leading *Muslim*s.

2   Recorded by Muslim. The Prophet's words in this *ḥadīth* are in al-Bukhārī as well.

> **(the highly virtuous) and the *shuhadā'* (martyrs).›"** [1]

Getting Up for *Qiyām*

Ablution and Cleaning the Teeth

As soon as he got up, the Prophet (ﷺ) would brush his teeth with *siwāk* [2] and perform *wuḍū'*. A number of such reports, narrated by 'Ā'ishah (R) and Ibn 'Abbās (ﷺ), will be cited in Chapter 6. Furthermore, 'Alī (ﷺ) reported that the Prophet (ﷺ) said:

> **‹When one of you gets up to pray at night, let him use *siwāk* (to clean his teeth), because when he recites during the prayer, an angel puts his mouth over his, so that nothing leaving his mouth but will enter into the angel's mouth.›** [3]

Mentioning Allāh

There are many *ḥadīth*s reporting things that the Prophet (ﷺ) said when he got up at night. In the following we list a few of them.

'Ubādah Bin aṣ-Ṣāmit (ﷺ) reported that the Prophet (ﷺ) said:

> **‹Whoever wakes up at night and says:**
>
> «لا إلٰه إلاّ اللّهُ وَحدَهُ لا شَريكَ له، له المُلكُ، وله الحمدُ، وهوَ على كل شيءٍ قَديرٌ، وسُبْحانَ اللّهِ، والحمدُ

1 Recorded by Ibn Khuzaymah, Ibn Ḥibbān, and others with an authentic *sanad* (chain of narrators).

2 A stick cut from the roots of a desert tree called *arāk*, and used to clean the teeth; it is also called *miswāk*. The act of cleaning the teeth with *siwāk* is called *tasawwuk*.

3 Recorded by al-Bayhaqī, aḍ-Ḍiyā', and others. Verified to be authentic by al-Albānī in *aṣ-Ṣaḥīḥah* no. 1213.

لِلَّهِ، ولا إلٰهَ إلاَّ اللَّهُ، واللَّهُ أكبرُ، ولا حوْلَ ولا قُوَّةَ إلاَّ باللَّهِ، ربِّ اغفِرْ لي»

"*Lā ilāha illallāhu waḥdahū lā sharīka lahū, lah ul-mulku wa-lah ul-ḥamdu wa-huwa 'alā kulli shay'in qadīr. Wa-subḥān allāhi, wal-ḥamdu lillāhi, wa-lā ilāha illāllāhu, wallāhu akbaru, wa-lā ḥawla wa-lā quwwata illā billāh.*" –

"There is no (true) god except Allāh, alone without any partners. To Him belongs the sovereignty; and to Him belongs all praise. He is capable of everything. Exalted is Allāh; all praise be to Allāh; there is no (true) god except Allāh; Allāh is the Greatest; there is no power or might except from Allāh," and then says, "*Rabb ighfir lī* – My Lord! Forgive me." Anyone who says this then supplicates, he will be answered; and if he makes *wuḍū'* and prays, his prayer will be accepted.⟩ [1]

Rabī'ah Bin Ka'b al-Aslamī (ﷺ) reported:

"I used to sleep by the house of the Prophet (ﷺ). When he got up at night (to pray), I would hear him repeat for a long time:

«سُبْحانَ ربِّ العالمينَ»

⟨*Subḥāna rabb il-'ālamīn* – Exalted is the Lord of the creation.⟩

Then he (ﷺ) would repeat for a long time:

«سُبْحانَ اللَّهِ وبحمْدِهِ»

⟨*Subḥān allāhi wa bi-ḥamdih* – Exalted is Allāh, all

---

1 Al-Bukhārī.

praise belongs to Him.»"[1]

Ibn 'Abbās (⌘) reported:

"The Prophet (⌘) sat up from sleep in the last third of the night, looked at the sky, and then recited, «*Inna fī khalq is-samāwāti wal-arḍi wakhtilāf il-layli wannahāri la āyātilli ulil-albāb ...* – **Verily, in the creation of the heavens and Earth, and the succession of night and day, are signs for those who have hearts ...**»[2] until he completed the *sūrah*."[3]

Voice Level

One may pray *qiyām* silently or aloud, but is best to raise his voice moderately. Abū Qatādah (⌘) reported that one night, the Prophet (⌘) saw Abū Bakr (⌘) praying with a low voice. He then saw 'Umar (⌘) praying with a loud voice. Afterwards, he (⌘) said to Abū Bakr, ‹**O Abū Bakr! I passed by you while you prayed, and you were lowering your voice.**› He replied, "I have been heard by Him whom I was addressing, O Allāh's Messenger!" Then the Prophet (⌘) said to 'Umar, ‹**O 'Umar! I passed by you while you prayed, and you were raising your voice.**› He replied, "O Allāh's Messenger! Thereby, I wake the sleepy and drive away Satan!" So the Prophet (⌘) said:

‹**O Abū Bakr, Raise your voice a little. And you 'Umar, lower your voice a little.**›[4]

Ibn 'Abbās (⌘) reported:

---

1   Recorded by an-Nasā'ī, at-Tirmithī, Abū 'Uwānah, and Muslim (in part). Verified to be authentic by al-Albānī.
2   *Āl 'Imrān* 3:190-200.
3   Al-Bukhārī and Muslim.
4   Recorded by Abū Dāwūd and at-Tirmithī. Verified to be authentic by al-Albānī.

"The Prophet's (ﷺ) recitation (in *qiyām*) was such that one would hear him from the outer room while he is inside (in the bedroom)." [1]

1 Recorded by Abū Dāwūd; al-Albānī verified it to be *ḥasan*.

CHAPTER 3

LAYLAT UL-QADR [1]

Meaning

The words *qadr* and *qadar* mean decree; *qadr* also means majesty or high esteem. [2] Thus, *Laylat ul-Qadr*, or the Night of *Qadr*, means the Night of Decree, or the Night of Majesty.

Merits

Laylat ul-Qadr is a very blessed night. It is the best night of *Ramaḍān*, rather, the whole year. Rewards for acts of worship during it are multiplied so as to equal one thousand months'. It is the night that Allāh (ﷻ) chose to send the *Qur'ān* down to the lowest heaven, from where it was revealed in small portions to Muḥammad (ﷺ).

It is the night on which Allāh (ﷻ) decrees His wise ordainments, appointing matters of life, death, sustenance, disasters, etc; and the angels descend with these decrees.

Allāh (ﷻ) says:

﴿إِنَّا أَنْزَلْنَاهُ فِي لَيْلَةِ ٱلْقَدْرِ۝ وَمَا أَدْرَاكَ مَا لَيْلَةُ ٱلْقَدْرِ۝
لَيْلَةُ ٱلْقَدْرِ خَيْرٌ مِنْ أَلْفِ شَهْرٍ۝ تَنَزَّلُ ٱلْمَلَائِكَةُ وَالرُّوحُ
فِيهَا بِإِذْنِ رَبِّهِم مِن كُلِّ أَمْرٍ۝ سَلَامٌ هِيَ حَتَّى مَطْلَعِ
ٱلْفَجْرِ۝﴾ القدر ١-٥

---

1 For the most part, this chapter is not from the work translated from al-Albānī, but was included here for the sake of completeness. The references used for this material are mentioned in the Preface.

2 *Lisān ul-ʿArab*.

«Verily! We have sent this (the *Qur'ān*) down in the Night of *al-Qadr*. And what will make you know what the Night of *al-Qadr* is? The Night of *al-Qadr* is better than one thousand months. In it the angels and the Spirit (Jibrīl) descend, by Allāh's permission, with all decrees. Peace it is, until the appearance of dawn.» [1]

And He (ﷻ) says:

﴿إِنَّا أَنْزَلْنَاهُ فِي لَيْلَةٍ مُبَارَكَةٍ إِنَّا كُنَّا مُنْذِرِينَ۝ فِيهَا يُفْرَقُ كُلُّ أَمْرٍ حَكِيمٍ۝ أَمْراً مِنْ عِنْدِنَا إِنَّا كُنَّا مُرْسِلِينَ۝ رَحْمَةً مِنْ رَبِّكَ إِنَّهُ هُوَ السَّمِيعُ الْعَلِيمُ۝﴾ الدخان ٣-٦

«Verily! We have sent this (the *Qur'ān*) down on a blessed night. Verily, We always warn (people from sinning). In it, every matter of ordainment is decreed – by Our command. Verily, We always send (the messengers for guidance). It is a mercy from Your Lord; He is indeed All-Hearing, All-Knowing.» [2]

It should be noted here that sending down the *Qur'ān* on *Laylat ul-Qadr* does not mean that it was revealed all at once to Muḥammad (ﷺ). According to the Scholars, it was sent down on that night from *al-Lawḥ ul-Maḥfūẓ* (the Preserved Tablet) to the lowest heaven. It was then revealed in small segments, as necessary, over a period of twenty three years of the Messenger's (ﷺ) life. [3]

The same applies to Allāh's decrees. They are not formulated on this specific night every year. Rather, Allāh (ﷻ), with His encompassing knowledge, knew all what will happen, and has recorded it all in *al-Lawḥ ul-Maḥfūẓ*. On *Laylat ul-Qadr*, Allāh (ﷻ) issues His

1 *Al-Qadr* 97:1-5.

2 *Ad-Dukhān* 44:3-5.

3 This is recorded in the books of *Tafsīr* from Ibn ʿAbbās, Qatādah, Ibn Zayd, and others. Review, for example, Ibn Kathīr's and al-Qurṭubī's.

decrees pertaining to the following year (life, death, sustenance, etc), after having been in *al-Lawḥ ul-Maḥfūẓ*, to the angels. [1]

Which Night?

Varying Reports and Opinions

There are various authentic *ḥadīth*s in which the Prophet (ﷺ) indicates that *Laylat ul-Qadr* falls on the night [2] of the twenty first, twenty third, twenty fifth, twenty seventh, twenty ninth, or last night of *Ramaḍān*. Because of this, the scholars have differed widely as to which night it actually falls on. Al-Ḥāfiẓ al-ʿIrāqī wrote a booklet on this subject, titled "*Sharḥ uṣ-Ṣadr bi-Thikri Laylat il-Qadr*", in which he covered all of the scholars' opinions in this regard. Imām ash-Shāfiʿī (r) said:

> "It seems to me that the Prophet (ﷺ) would answer in accordance with the question. So if one asked him, 'Should we seek it on such and such night?' He would reply, 'Yes, seek it on such and such night.' " [3]

The Last Ten Nights of *Ramaḍān*

The various reports indicate that *Laylat ul-Qadr* definitely falls on the last ten nights of *Ramaḍān*, and most frequently on the last seven nights, as in Ibn ʿUmar's report that the Prophet (ﷺ) said:

> **‹Seek it on the last ten nights. If one of you is weak, let him not miss (at least) the last seven nights.›** [4]

---

1 This meaning is recorded in the books of *Tafsīr* from Ibn ʿAbbās, Qatādah, Mujāhid, al-Ḥasan, and others. Review, for example, Ibn Kathīr's and al-Qurṭubī's.

2 "The night of the twenty-first" means the night preceding the twenty-first day of *Ramaḍān*.

3 Reported by al-Baghawī in *Sharḥ us-Sunnah* (6:388).

4 Al-Bukhārī and Muslim.

The knowledge of the exact night on which it falls is hidden from the Muslims. ʿUbādah Bin aṣ-Ṣāmit (ﷺ) reported that the Prophet (ﷺ) walked into the *Masjid* (Prophet's mosque) and found two men arguing. He said:

> **‹I was coming to tell you about (the time of) *Laylat ul-Qadr*; when such and such men disputed, the knowledge of this was raised (taken); and this may be better for you. So seek it on the ninth, seventh, and fifth nights (after twenty).›** [1]

THE NIGHT OF THE TWENTY-FIRST

In another report, Abū Saʿīd al-Khudrī (ﷺ) narrates that a number of the *ṣaḥābah* performed *iʿtikāf* with Allāh's Messenger (ﷺ) during the middle ten days of *Ramaḍān*. On the morning of the twentieth of *Ramaḍān*, they were preparing to leave when the Prophet (ﷺ) addressed them saying:

> **‹I was informed (by Allāh) about (when is) *Laylat ul-Qadr*. But I was then made to forget it. So seek it on the last ten, on an odd night. I was also informed that I will make *sujūd* [2] (for the morning prayer that follows it) in water and mud. So let those who started *iʿtikāf* with Allāh's Messenger return (to the *Masjid* for ten more days of *iʿtikāf*).›**

Abū Saʿīd then continues:

> "The people went back to the *Masjid* (to resume *iʿtikāf*). We could not see even a thin cloud in the sky. But then, a large cloud came; and it rained that night.

1 Al-Bukhārī.

2 *Sujūd*: Prostration during the prayer, which involves putting the forehead and nose on the ground. This derives from the verb *sajada*. And from this is the word *masjid* as well, which means a place for *sujūd* or worship.

> The roof of the *Masjid*, which was made of palm reeds, leaked in the Messenger's prayer place on the night of the twenty-first. The (morning) prayer was performed; and Allāh's Messenger (ﷺ) made *sujūd* in mud and water, until I saw the mud on his nose and forehead." [1]

The Night of the Twenty-seventh

Other *ḥadīths* indicate that *Laylat ul-Qadr* falls on the twenty-seventh night of *Ramaḍān*. For example, Zirr Bin Ḥubaysh reported that Ubayy Bin Kaʿb was informed that Ibn Masʿūd said, "Whoever stands the whole year (in prayer), he will certainly encounter *Laylat ul-Qadr*." Upon hearing this, Ubayy (رضي الله عنه) said:

> "May Allāh have mercy on him, he did not want the people to become lazy (if they new more precisely when it is). By the One whom there is no deity but Him, it is surely in *Ramaḍān*. I swear by Allāh I know which night it is: It is the night in which Allāh's Messenger (ﷺ) commanded us to stand (in prayer); it is the night preceding the morning of the twenty-seventh (of *Ramaḍān*). Its sign is that the sun rises the following morning white and without rays." [2]

Summary

Therefore, *Laylat ul-Qadr* falls on an odd night of the last ten nights of *Ramaḍān*; it is more likely to be on the last seven, and most likely on the middle one of those, which is the night of the twenty-seventh.

The scholars differ as to whether it always comes on a fixed night, namely, the twenty-seventh [3], as in Zirr's *ḥadīth*, or moves from year to year between these nights [4]. The safest approach is to follow the

1 Al-Bukhārī.

2 Muslim and others.

3 This is the opinion expressed by al-Albānī in *Qiyāmu Ramaḍān*.

4 This is ash-Shawkānī's opinion in *Nayl ul-Awṭār*.

ḥadīths instructing one to seek it at least on the odd nights of the last ten. At the same time, special care should be given to the night of the twenty-seventh, because it is the night on which the Prophet (ﷺ) gathered all of his family, and passed it in prayer and worship, as in the forthcoming *ḥadīth* of Abū Tharr (p. 34).

How to Seek *Laylat ul-Qadr*

Laylat ul-Qadr is the most blessed night. A person who misses it has indeed missed a great amount of good. If a believing person is zealous to obey his Lord and increase the good deeds in his record, he should strive to encounter this night and to pass it in worship and obedience. If this is facilitated for him, all of his previous sins will be forgiven.

PRAYING *QIYĀM*

It is recommended to make a long *Qiyām* prayer during the nights on which *Laylat ul-Qadr* could fall. This is indicated in many *ḥadīths*, such as the forthcoming one by Abū Tharr (p. 34). Furthermore, Abū Hurayrah (ﷺ) narrated that the Messenger (ﷺ) said:

> **‹Whoever stands (in *qiyām*) in *Laylat ul-Qadr* [and it is facilitated for him][1] out of faith and expectation (of Allāh's reward), will have all of his previous sins forgiven.›** [2]

MAKING SUPPLICATIONS

It is also recommended to make extensive supplication on this night. 'Ā'ishah (R) reported that she asked Allāh's Messenger (ﷺ), "O Messenger of Allāh! If I knew which night is *Laylat ul-Qadr*, what

1 This addition is recorded by Aḥmad from the report of 'Ubādah Bin aṣ-Ṣāmit; it means that he is permitted to be among the sincere worshippers during that blessed night.

2 Al-Bukhārī and Muslim.

should I say during it?" And he instructed her to say:

«اللَّهُمَّ إِنَّكَ عَفُوٌّ تُحِبُّ ٱلعَفْوَ فَاعْفُ عَنِّي»

‹*Allāhumma innaka ʿafuwwun tuḥibb ul-ʿafwa faʿfu ʿannī* – O Allāh! You are forgiving, and you love forgiveness. So forgive me.› [1]

Abandoning Worldly Pleasures for the Sake of Worship

It is further recommended to spend more time in worship during the nights on which *Laylat ul-Qadr* is likely to be. This calls for abandoning many worldly pleasures in order to secure the time and thoughts solely for worshipping Allāh. ʿĀ'ishah (R) reported:

> "When the (last) ten started, the Prophet (ﷺ) would tighten his *izār* [2], spend the whole night awake (in prayer), and wake up his family." [3]

And she said:

> "Allāh's Messenger (ﷺ) used to exert more (in worship) on the last ten than on other nights." [4]

Signs of *Laylat ul-Qadr*

Authentic Signs

There are signs, mentioned in the authentic reports, by which one

---

1 Recorded by Aḥmad, Ibn Mājah, and at-Tirmithī. Verified to be authentic by al-Albānī.

2 This means that he stayed away from his wives in order to have more time for worship.

3 Al-Bukhārī and Muslim.

4 Muslim.

might be able to tell whether a specific night was *Laylat ul-Qadr* or not. It is interesting to note that these signs occur after the night ends. Some scholars have indicated that the wisdom behind this is that one would not rely on definite knowledge in order to limit his worship to just one night of the whole year. This understanding is supported by the Prophet's (ﷺ) statement in the preceding *ḥadīth* of 'Ubādah, **‹... And this may be better for you. ›**.

In the preceding *ḥadīth* of Ubayy, he (ﷺ) said, "Its sign is that the sun rises on the following morning white, and without rays." Similarly, Abū Tharr (ﷺ) reported that the Prophet (ﷺ) said:

> **‹On the morning following *Laylat ul-Qadr*, the sun rises without rays, resembling a dish, until it becomes high.›** [1]

Abū Sa'īd's preceding *ḥadīth* indicates that it is a humid or rainy night. A *ḥadīth* reported by Ibn 'Abbās informs that it is a moderate night, neither hot nor cold. [2]

According to some scholars, the last two descriptions apply to the particular years when the Prophet (ﷺ) made his statements.

UNFOUNDED FOLK-TALES

Many fables circulate among the common people, claiming unusual incidents happening during *Laylat ul-Qadr*. These fables claim that the trees make *sujūd*, animals act, in a strange way, sinners who happen to wake up for a few seconds and ask for wealth become millionaires, etc ...

All of this is nonsense! *Laylat ul-Qadr* is a blessed night which should be spent in worship and obedience, not in negligence or sinning. Only the one who makes good use of it, in accordance with the *Sunnah*, as outlined above, can hope for Allāh's acceptance and blessings.

---

1 Muslim.

2 Recorded by Ibn Khuzaymah and others. Its *isnād* is *ḥasan*.

CHAPTER 4

PRAYING *TARĀWĪḤ* IN *JAMĀʿAH*

The Prophet's *Sunnah*

It is recommended to pray the *qiyām* of *Ramaḍān* in *jamāʿah* (congregation); and it is better than praying it individually. The Prophet (ﷺ) himself established it: he (ﷺ) approved of it from the *ṣaḥābah* (ﷺ), did it himself, and emphasized its merits.

The Prophet's Approval

This approval is indicated in the *ḥadīth* of Thaʿlabah Bin Abū Mālik al-Quraẓī, who said:

> "Allāh's Messenger (ﷺ) went out (to the *Masjid*) one night during *Ramaḍān*; he saw some people in the corner of the *Masjid* praying. He asked, ‹**What are they doing?**› Someone replied, 'O Allāh's Messenger, these people do not know much *Qurʾān*; Ubayy Bin Kaʿb is reciting; and they are behind him following his prayer.' To which he (ﷺ) replied, ‹**They have done well,**› or he said, ‹**They have done right,**› and he did not object to their action." [1]

The Prophet's Action

There are various *ḥadīth*s indicating that the Prophet (ﷺ) prayed

1 Recorded by al-Bayhaqī (2:495). It is *mursal* (no *ṣaḥābī*'s name is mentioned in the chain), Thaʿlabah being a *tābiʿī* (student of the *ṣaḥābah*; plural *tābiʿīn* or *tābiʿūn*). But it is recorded with another *isnād* from Abū Hurayrah (ﷺ) by Ibn Naṣr al-Marwazī (in *Qiyām ul-Layl*), Abū Dāwūd, and al-Bayhaqī. This report is acceptable as a supportive report.

tarāwīḥ in *jamāʿah.*

1. An-Nuʿmān Bin Bashīr (ﷺ) reported:

> "We stood (in prayer) with Allāh's Messenger (ﷺ) on the twenty third night of *Ramaḍān* up to the first third of the night; then we stood with him on the twenty-fifth night up to the middle of the night; then he led us on the twenty-seventh night (for so long) that we feared missing the *falāḥ* (success) ... We used to call *saḥūr* [1]: *falāḥ*." [2]

Commenting on this *ḥadīth*, al-Ḥākim said:

> "This carries a clear proof that praying *tarāwīḥ* in the *masjids* of Muslims is an established *sunnah*; ʿAlī Bin Abī Ṭālib (ﷺ) continued to urge ʿUmar (ﷺ) to revive it, until he finally did." [3]

2. Anas (ﷺ) reported:

> "Allāh's Messenger (ﷺ) was praying in *Ramaḍān*. So I went and stood next to him; then someone else came, then someone else – until there was a small group. When Allāh's Messenger (ﷺ) realized that we were all praying behind him, he made his prayer short, then he entered his house. Inside his house, he (ﷺ) resumed praying a much longer prayer than that he prayed with us. In the morning we said, 'O Allāh's Messenger, did you notice our presence last night?' He replied, **‹Yes, and this is the reason for what I did.›** " [4]

---

1 A light meal eaten by the fasting person just before dawn.

2 Recorded by Ibn Abī Shaybah (in *al-Muṣannaf*), Ibn Naṣr, an-Nasāʾī, Aḥmad, al-Faryābī (in *Kitāb uṣ-Ṣiyām*), and al-Ḥākim; its *isnād* is *ṣaḥīḥ*.

3 *Al-Mustadrak* 1:440.

4 Recorded by Aḥmad, Ibn Naṣr with two authentic chains, and at-Ṭabarānī in *al-*

3. ʿĀ'ishah (R) reported:

"The people used to pray during *Ramaḍān*'s nights in the Messenger's *Masjid* in separate groups. Thus, a man who knew some *Qur'ān* would have five or six people praying behind him.

On one such night, the Messenger of Allāh (ﷺ) instructed me to lay down a mat for him (in the *Masjid*) by the door of my apartment; so I did. After praying *ʿishā'*, Allāh's Messenger (ﷺ) went to that mat (to pray). All those who were in the *Masjid* gathered behind him; and he (ﷺ) led them in prayer for a long portion of the night; then he (ﷺ) departed and entered (my apartment), leaving the mat where it was.

In the morning, the people described that Allāh's Messenger (ﷺ) led some men in prayer on the previous night. So that night, more people gathered, until the *Masjid* was full. Allāh's Messenger (ﷺ) went out the second night and prayed; and they followed him in the prayer.

The next morning, the people talked about it. So, on the third night, the number of people increased in the *Masjid* [until it became overcrowded with them]. Again, Allāh's Messenger (ﷺ) went out; and they followed him in the prayer.

On the fourth night the *Masjid* was overrun with people. Allāh's Messenger (ﷺ) prayed *ʿishā'* with them, then he went inside his house. But the people remained; so Allāh's Messenger (ﷺ) asked me, **‹What do they want, ʿĀ'ishah?›** I said, 'O Allāh's Messenger! The people have heard of your prayer yesterday, and have gathered to follow you.' He (ﷺ) said, **‹Fold away your mat,›** which I did.

That night, Allāh's Messenger (ﷺ) was aware of the people in their places, waiting for him. Some men

---

Āwsaṭ.

among them were calling out, 'The Prayer!'

In the morning, Allāh's Messenger (ﷺ) went out to the *fajr* [1] prayer. After he finished praying, he turned to the people, said the *Shahādah* [2], and then said:

‹O people, by Allāh, and all praise is due to Him, I was not unaware of your presence last night, but I only feared that the night prayer (*qiyām*) would become an obligation for you, which you would be incapable of fulfilling. So commit only to the deed that you would be capable of performing, because Allāh would not tire (from a deed of yours) until you tire.›"

In one of the narrations of this *ḥadīth*, az-Zuhrī [3] said:

"Allāh's Messenger (ﷺ) died while the people continued according to this (praying *tarāwīḥ* in separate groups). This also continued during the *khilāfah* of Abū Bakr and a portion of the *khilāfah* of 'Umar." [4]

According to al-Ḥāfiẓ Ibn Ḥajar:

"The statement 'the people continued according to this' refers to not praying *tarāwīḥ* in *jamā'ah*."

However, it is better to interpret the statement as, "They continued

1 *Fajr*: The morning or dawn prayer, which is the first of the five obligatory prayers. Its time extends from dawn until sunrise.

2 The Prophet's (ﷺ) *sunnah* was to start his talks with *Khuṭbat ul-Ḥājah* (the Testimony of Need). This is sometimes referred to as *tashahhud* (saying the *Shahādah*) because the *Shahādah* (testifying that there is no god except Allāh and that Muḥammad is His Messenger) is an important part of it.

3 A *tābi'ī* who reported from 'Ā'ishah.

4 Al-Bukhārī, Muslim, Abū Dāwūd, an-Nasā'ī, al-Faryābī, Ibn Naṣr, and Aḥmad. The above text agrees most with the reports of the latter two.

to pray *tarāwīḥ* in separate groups," as the beginning of this *ḥadīth* indicates. Thus, they continued to pray behind various *imāms*, as will be confirmed further in the reports from ʿUmar (ﷺ).

These *ḥadīths* provide clear evidence for praying *tarāwīḥ* in *jamāʿah*, since the Prophet (ﷺ) prayed it on those nights. This conclusion does not conflict with his stopping on the fourth night, because he stated the reason for his action, **‹I feared that it would become obligatory for you.›**

And there is no doubt that this apprehension dissipated with his (ﷺ) passing after Allāh (ﷻ) had completed the religion. Thus, the reason for not praying *tarāwīḥ* in congregation was gone, restoring the earlier ruling that it is recommended to pray it in *jamāʿah*. This is why ʿUmar Bin al-Khaṭ ṭāb (ﷺ) revived it, as is the opinion of the majority of the scholars.

4. Ḥuthayfah Bin al-Yamān (ﷺ) reported:

> "One night during *Ramaḍān*, Allāh's Messenger (ﷺ) stood in a cabin made of palm reeds. He poured a pail of water on himself, then said, **‹*Allāhu Akbar* – Allāh is the Greatest [three times]; *Thal malakūti, wal jabarūti, wal kibrīyāʾi, wal ʿaẓamah* – You are the Possessor of dominion, might, pride, and greatness.›** Then he recited *al-Baqarah*; then he bowed a bowing similar (in duration) to his standing. During his bowing he said, **‹*Subḥāna rabbiyal ʿaẓīm, subḥāna rabbiyal ʿaẓīm* – exalted is my Lord the Great; exalted is my Lord the Great.›** Then he raised his head from bowing, and stood (a duration) similar to his bowing, saying, **‹*Lirabbīyal ḥamd* – to my Lord belong the praise.›** Then he prostrated, and his prostration was similar (in duration) to his (last) standing. He was saying in his prostration, **‹*Subḥāna rabbiyal aʿlā* – exalted is my Lord the Highest.›** Then he raised his head from prostration and sat; and he said between the two prostrations: **‹*Rabbighfir lī, rabbighfir lī* – my Lord, forgive me; my Lord, forgive me.›** And he sat a

> duration similar to that of his prostration. Then he prostrated (a second time) and said, ‹***Subḥāna rabbiyal a'lā,***› similar (in duration) to his sitting. Thus he prayed four *rak'āt*, reciting in them *al-Baqarah*, *Āl-'Imrān*, *an-Nisā'*, *al-Mā'idah*, and *al-An'ām* - until Bilāl came announcing the time for the (*fajr*) prayer."[1]

The Prophet's Encouragement

The Prophet (ﷺ) indicated the merits of praying *tarāwīḥ* in *jamā'ah.* For example, Abū Tharr (رضي الله عنه) reported the following:

> "We fasted with Allāh's Messenger (ﷺ) in *Ramaḍān*. He did not lead us (in *qiyām*) at all until there were seven (nights of *Ramaḍān*) left. Then he stood with us (that night – in prayer) until one third of the night had passed. He did not pray with us on the sixth. On the fifth night, he prayed with us until half of the night had passed. So we said, 'Allāh's Messenger! Wouldn't you pray with us the whole night?' He replied:
>
> **‹Whoever stands in prayer with the *imām* until he (the *imām*) concludes the prayer, it is recorded for him that he prayed the whole night.›**
>
> He (ﷺ) did not lead us in prayer on the fourth (of the remaining nights). On the third night[2], he gathered his family, his wives and the people. He led us in prayer (for a long time) - until we feared missing the *falāḥ*. He (ﷺ) did not pray with us for the rest of the month."

1 Recorded (in various parts and with some variations) by Muslim, Aḥmad, Abū Dāwūd, an-Nasā'ī, at-Tirmithī, Ibn Mājah, Ibn Abī Shaybah, Ibn Naṣr, al-Ḥākim, at-Ṭaḥāwī in (*al-Mushkal*), aṭ-Ṭayālisī, al-Bayhaqī, and al-Baghawī.

2 Meaning the twenty-seventh night, which is *Laylat ul-Qadr* according to most sayings. This is why the Prophet (ﷺ) gathered all of his family and women, which makes it desirable that the women attend on this night.

Abū Tharr was asked, "What is *falāḥ*?" He replied, "*Saḥūr*." [1]

The evidence from this *ḥadīth* is his (ﷺ) statement, **‹Whoever stands with the *imām* ...›** which is an obvious indication that it is better to pray the *qiyām* of *Ramaḍān* with the *imām*. This is confirmed by what Abū Dāwūd mentioned:

> "I heard Aḥmad being asked, 'Do you like for a man to pray with the people or by himself during *Ramaḍān*?' He replied, 'Pray with the people.' I also heard him say, 'I would prefer for one to pray (*qiyām*) with the *imām* and to pray *witr* with him as well, for the Prophet (ﷺ) said: **‹When a man prays with the *imām* until he concludes, it is recorded that he prayed the rest of that night.›**" [2]

Ibn Naṣr reported similarly from Aḥmad. Abū Dāwūd also said:

> "Aḥmad was asked, while I was listening, 'Should one delay *qiyām*, meaning *tarāwīḥ*, to the last part of the night?' He said, 'No, the Muslims' *Sunnah* is more beloved to me.'" [3]

By this he meant that praying *tarāwīḥ* in *jamāʿah*, early in the night, is better than praying it alone later in the night. Even though delaying it has a special merit, yet praying it in *jamāʿah* is better because the Prophet (ﷺ) established it on those nights when he prayed with the people, as in the preceding *ḥadīths* of ʿĀ'ishah and others. That is why the Muslims continued to do it from ʿUmar's time until now.

---

1 Recorded by Ibn Abī Shaybah, Abū Dāwūd, at-Tirmithī (who authenticated it), an-Nisā'ī, Ibn Mājah, at-Ṭaḥawī (in *Sharḥu Maʿān il-Āthār*, Ibn Naṣr, al-Faryābī, and al-Bayhaqī. Their *isnād* is authentic.

2 *Al-Masā'il*.

3 *Al-Masā'il*.

REASON FOR DISCONTINUING *QIYĀM* IN *JAMĀʿAH*

As indicated in the preceding *ḥadīth* of ʿĀʾishah (R) in the Two *Ṣaḥīḥs* and others, the Prophet (ﷺ) did not pray with the *ṣaḥābah* for the remainder of the month, fearing that the *qiyām* prayer in *Ramaḍān* would become obligatory for them, an obligation that they would not be able to fulfill.

This apprehension dissolved with his (ﷺ) passing after Allāh (ﷻ) had completed the religion. Thus, the reason for not praying the *qiyām* of *Ramaḍān* in congregation was gone, though the earlier ruling of its merit remained intact.

The practice of praying it in *jamāʿah* was then revived by ʿUmar (رضي الله عنه), as is described below.

ʿUmar Revives the *Sunnah*

ʿUMAR'S ACTION

As mentioned above, after the Prophet's (ﷺ) death, people prayed *tarāwīḥ* in the *Masjid* in separate groups, behind various *imāms*. That was during the *Khilāfah* of Abū Bakr (رضي الله عنه) and a portion of ʿUmar's (رضي الله عنه). Later on, ʿUmar (رضي الله عنه) gathered the people behind one *imām*. Abd ur-Raḥmān Bin Abd al-Qārī reported:

> "I went out with ʿUmar Bin al-Khaṭ ṭāb (رضي الله عنه) one night in *Ramaḍān* to the *Masjid*; we found the people praying in separate groups: a man praying by himself, or a man leading a group of people in the prayer. So he (رضي الله عنه) said, 'By Allāh (ﷻ), I believe that it would be better if I gather all of these people behind one reciter only.' Later on, he resolved to do it, and gathered them behind Ubayy Bin Kaʿb.
>
> I went out with him on another night while the people were praying behind one reciter. ʿUmar (رضي الله عنه) said, 'This is indeed a good new practice, even though the part of night that they sleep through is better (for

> prayer) than the part in which they are praying.' By that, he meant the later part of the night, because the people used to pray early in the night." [1]

This has another report in which 'Umar (ﷺ) says:

> "If this thing is innovated, then it is indeed a good innovation." [2]

'Umar's Understanding

Thus, as indicated earlier, the Prophet (ﷺ) led the *ṣaḥābah* in *tarāwīḥ* for three nights; then he stopped for fear that this prayer would become an obligation on the Muslims. The people then continued to pray in small groups, as they did before, until 'Umar gathered them, may Allāh (ﷻ) be pleased with him and reward him for his great efforts for *Islām*. Ibn ut-Tīn and other scholars concluded:

> "'Umar (ﷺ) deduced that he should do this from the Prophet's (ﷺ) approval during those nights. When he (ﷺ) later disliked it, it was only because he feared that it would become obligatory for the people. It is probably for this reason that al-Bukhārī, after mentioning 'Umar's action, cited 'Ā'ishah's *ḥadīth* (which preceded). After the Prophet (ﷺ) passed away, such fear was gone, and 'Umar realized the importance of gathering the people, because praying separately gives the appearance of disunity, and because praying behind one *imām* helps the people endure the length of

---

1 This is recorded by Mālik (in *al-Muwṭṭa'*) and, from him, al-Bukhārī and al-Faryābī. It is also recorded by Ibn Abī Shaybah without his saying, "This is a good new matter."

2 Recorded by Ibn Sa'd and al-Faryābī. The narrators of this report are all trustworthy, except Nawfal Bin Iyās, about whom al-Ḥāfiẓ said (in *at-Taqrīb*), "Acceptable," meaning when he is backed by other narrators; otherwise he is weak, as al-Ḥāfiẓ himself stated in the introduction.

> the prayer. This action of ʿUmar was adopted by the majority of the scholars (as being the truth)." [1]

In regard to ʿUmar's (ﷺ) statement, "The part of night that they sleep through is better," al-Ḥāfiẓ Ibn Ḥajar said:

> "This is a declaration from him that praying during the later part of the night is better than praying early. However, It does not imply that praying the night prayer (*tarāwīḥ*) individually is better than in *jamāʿah*."

In fact, praying in *jamāʿah* at the earlier time is surely better than praying individually at the later time, as has been clarified earlier.

Wrong Conclusions from ʿUmar's Action

A common practice among people of the later generations is to misinterpret ʿUmar's (ﷺ) statement, "*Niʿmat il-bidʿatu hāthih* – This is indeed a good new matter." Many use it as basis for two misconceptions:

First Misconception:

> "Praying *tarāwīḥ* in *jamāʿah* is a *bidʿah* that was not known during the time of the Prophet (ﷺ)."

The error of this misconception is obvious, as is demonstrated in the *ḥadīths* that we cited earlier: The Prophet (ﷺ) prayed with the people in *jamāʿah* for three nights in *Ramaḍān*; and he only stopped for fear that it would become an obligation.

Second Misconception:

> "Some *bidʿahs* (innovations) are praiseworthy; and general statements by the Prophet (ﷺ), such as, ‹**Every**

1 *Fatḥ ul-Bārī* 4:203-204.

> ***bidʿah* is an act of misguidance›** should be restricted by this statement of ʿUmar."

This is also invalid. The general meaning of this and similar *ḥadīth*s holds without restriction.

In his statement, ʿUmar did not intend the *sharʿī* (legislative) meaning of *bidʿah*, which is to innovate in the *Dīn* something without a precedent. It is clear that he did not innovate anything, but has rather revived several of the Prophet's (ﷺ) *sunnah*s.

He only meant *bidʿah* according to one of its linguistic meanings, which is a new or novel thing that was not commonly known prior to its initiation. There is no doubt that praying *tarāwīḥ* in *jamāʿah* behind one *imām* was not a commonly known practice during the *Khilāfah* of Abū Bakr (رضي الله عنه) and a portion of ʿUmar's (رضي الله عنه), as preceded. With this understanding, it is a new matter. But since it is in accordance with the Prophet's (ﷺ) action, it is a *sunnah* and not *bidʿah*. Describing it as being good is only because of this; and this is the understanding of the great scholars in explanation of this statement by ʿUmar. For example, Abd ul-Wahhāb as-Sụbkī said:

> "Ibn ʿAbd ul-Barr said, 'ʿUmar did not legislate except what Allāh's Messenger legislated, and what he loved and accepted. Nothing prevented him (ﷺ) from continuing (with *tarāwīḥ* in *jamāʿah*) except fearing that it would become an obligation for his *Ummah* (nation or followers), because he was kind and merciful toward the believers. ʿUmar (رضي الله عنه) learned that from Allāh's Messenger (ﷺ), and understood that one may not add to the obligations or take away from them after his (ﷺ) death. He therefore re-established it for the people, revived it, and commanded it; he did this on the year fourteen of *Hijrah*. That was a (good) thing that Allāh reserved for him particularly to do; He (ﷻ) did not inspire Abū Bakr (رضي الله عنه) to do it, even though he was better than him, and generally faster in performing all that is good. Each of these two possessed virtues that his companion did not.'

Had *tarāwīḥ* not been an ordained *sunnah*, it would be a rejected innovation, as is the case for *ar-Raghā'ib* prayer on the middle night of *Sha'bān* and on the first Friday of *Rajab*. If this was the case, it would be incumbent to forbid it; but that was never done, as is obviously known in the *Dīn*." [1]

The great scholar Ibn Ḥajar al-Haythamī said:

"Driving the Jews and Christians out of the Arabian peninsula, and fighting the Turks are not *bid'ahs* – since these were done by the command of the Prophet (ﷺ), even though they were not done during his lifetime. And in 'Umar's saying regarding the *tarāwīḥ* prayers, 'This is indeed a good *bid'ah*,' he meant the linguistic meaning of *bid'ah*, which is to do something that was not being done, similar to what Allāh (ﷻ) says:

﴿قُلْ مَا كُنْتُ بِدْعًا مِنَ ٱلرُّسُلِ﴾ الأحقاف ٩

«I did not bring something unprecedented among the messengers.» [2]

This does not indicate a *bid'ah* in the *shar'ī* sense, because such a *bid'ah* would be an act of misguidance, as was indicated by the Messenger (ﷺ).

Scholars who classify the *bid'ahs* into good and bad only intend the linguistic meaning of *bid'ahs*; and those who say that every *bid'ah* is a misguidance mean the *bid'ah* in the *shar'ī* sense.

Just look at how the *ṣaḥābah* (ﷺ), as well as those who followed them in a good way, have objected to giving *aṯẖān* for prayers other than the five daily

1 *Ishrāq ul-Maṣābīḥ fī Ṣalāt it-Tarāwīḥ* (1:168).

2 *Al-Aḥqāf* 46:9.

prayers, such as the *'Īd* prayers, even though there is no explicit prohibition in that regard. Also, they disliked people holding onto the two *Shāmī* [1] corners of the *Ka'bah,* as well as praying after *sa'ī* [2] in analogy to praying after *ṭawāf* (circulation around al-Ka'bah).

Furthermore, there are things that the Prophet (ﷺ) avoided despite the need and ability to do them during his lifetime. Avoiding such things is then a *sunnah*, and doing them is a blameworthy innovation. By our saying, 'Despite the need and ability to do them,' we exclude driving out the Jews, compiling the *Muṣḥaf*, and other things that he (ﷺ) did not do because of reasons that prevented doing them.

Thus, there was a need to pray *tarāwīḥ* in *jamā'ah*, but there was also a reason that prevented the Prophet (ﷺ) from continuing to pray it in *jamā'ah*." [3]

Women Joining the *Jamā'ah*

Women are permitted to attend the *qiyām* prayer, as is indicated in the preceding *ḥadīth* of Abū Tharr. It is also permitted to appoint an *imām* specifically for them. It is confirmed that 'Umar (ﷺ) gathered the people for *qiyām*, appointing Ubayy Bin Ka'b to lead the men, and Sulaymān Bin Abī Ḥathmah to lead the women. Also, 'Arfajah ath-Thaqafī said:

> "'Alī Bin Abī Ṭālib (ﷺ) commanded the people to pray *qiyām* during the month of *Ramaḍān*; he appointed one *imām* for the men and one for the women. I was the women's *imām*." [4]

---

1 These are the two corners on the north side of the *Ka'bah*, which is the direction of the land of ash-Shām (Syria, Lebanon, Jordan, and Palestine).

2 Running between aṣ-Ṣafā and al-Marwah during *ḥajj*.

3 *Al-Ibdā' fī Maḍārr il-Ibtidā'*.

4 These two reports were recorded by al-Bayhaqī, 'Abd ur-Razāq (in *al-Muṣannaf*),

This is recommended when the *masjid* is large enough that the two *imāms* would not distract each other (by their recitation).

---

and Ibn Naṣr (in *Qiyām ul-Layl*).

CHAPTER 5

NUMBER OF *RAKʿĀT* FOR *QIYĀM*

Introduction

The correct number of *rakʿāt* for *qiyām* is eleven (11). This follows from the Messenger's (ﷺ) *Sunnah.* One may not add to this number, for he (ﷺ) did not add to it his entire life.

However, one may reduce the number of these *rakʿāt*; one may even pray only one *rakʿah* of *witr.* This is supported by the Prophet's (ﷺ) actions and words.

The Number that the Prophet Prayed

We have established that it is recommended to pray *tarāwīḥ* in *jamāʿah.* We need next to establish the number of *rakʿāt* that the Prophet (ﷺ) performed when he prayed alone, as well as when he led the people in *jamāʿah.*

ʿĀ'ISHAH'S REPORTS

Abū Salamah Bin ʿAbd ur-Raḥmān reported that he asked ʿĀ'ishah (R) about the Messenger's prayer during *Ramaḍān.* She said:

> "Whether it was *Ramaḍān* or any other month, Allāh's Messenger (ﷺ) did not pray more than eleven *rakʿāt.* He would pray four [1] - and do not ask about their beauty or length. Then he would pray four - and do not ask about their beauty or length. Then he would pray three." [2]

1 Meaning with one *taslīm.*

2 Recorded by al-Bukhārī, Muslim, Abū ʿUwānah, Abū Dāwūd, at-Tirmiḏhī, an-

An-Nawawī commented in his Explanation of *Ṣaḥīḥ Muslim*, "This indicates the permission to do so (pray four with one *taslīm*). However, it is better to perform *taslīm* every two *rakʿāt*, which was the common practice of the Prophet (ﷺ), and conforms with his command to pray the night prayer in pairs."

The position in the *Shāfiʿī ma<u>th</u>hab*, as indicated in *al-Fiqhu ʿalal Ma<u>th</u>āhib il-Arbaʿah*, al-Qasṭalāni's Commentary on *al-Bukhārī*, and others is, "One must make *taslīm* at the end of each pair of *rakʿāt*; and if one prays the four with one *taslīm*, his prayer will not be acceptable." This position conflicts with this authentic *ḥadīth*, as well as the above sound understanding of an-Nawawī, who is one of the great scholars of that *ma<u>th</u>hab*. Thus, no one is excused to give a *fatwā* (verdict) contrary to this.

In another report, ʿĀ'ishah (R) said:

> "Allāh's Messenger (ﷺ) prayed at night, in *Ramaḍān* and other months, thirteen *rakʿāt*, of which were the two *rakʿāt* of *fajr*." [1]

And in still another report, ʿĀ'ishah (R) said:

> "Allāh's Messenger (ﷺ) prayed thirteen *rakʿāt* at night. Then, after hearing the call for *fajr* prayer, he would pray two short *rakʿāt*." [2]

Regarding the apparent conflict between the last two reports, al-Ḥāfiẓ Ibn Ḥajar said:

> "It is possible that, in this report, ʿĀ'ishah included in the night prayer the two post-*ʿishā'* *rakʿāt* that he (ﷺ) prayed at home, or the two short *rakʿāt* with which he (ﷺ) started the *qiyām*. It is established in *Ṣaḥīḥ Muslim* that he (ﷺ) used to start his night prayer with

---

Nasā'ī, Mālik, al-Bayhaqī, and Aḥmad.

1 Recorded by Ibn Abī Shaybah, Muslim, and others.

2 Recorded by Mālik and, from him, al-Bukhārī and others.

> two short *rakʿāt*. I find the latter possibility more correct, because the report of Abū Salamah, which confines the number to eleven *rakʿāt*, describes that, 'He prayed four then four then three.' It does not make any reference to the two short *rakʿāt* mentioned in Mālik's report. This is permissible, because the addition to a report by a meticulous reporter (*ḥāfiẓ*) is acceptable. This is further confirmed by a report recorded by Aḥmad and Abū Dāwūd from ʿAbdullāh Bin Abī Qays from ʿĀ'ishah saying:
>
> 'The Prophet (ﷺ) would make *witr* with four and three, ..., or ten and three. He would not make *witr* with more than thirteen or less than seven' [1]
>
> This is the most authentic report that I found in this regard, and with it, one may resolve the apparent conflict between the reports from ʿĀ'ishah."

This explanation by al-Ḥāfiẓ is also confirmed by Mālik's report from Zayd Bin Khālid al-Juhanī who narrated:

> "One night, I decided to closely observe the way the Messenger (ﷺ) performed his night prayer.
> So he prayed two short *rakʿāt*.
> Then he prayed two extremely long *rakʿāt*.
> Then he prayed two *rakʿāt* shorter than the preceding two.
> Then he prayed two *rakʿāt* shorter than the preceding two.
> Then he prayed two *rakʿāt* shorter than the preceding two.
> Then he prayed two *rakʿāt* shorter than the preceding two.
> Then he prayed (one) *witr*.
> This made thirteen *rakʿāt*." [2]

What seems to be most likely is that these two short *rakʿāt* are the

1 This *ḥadīth* will be cited later in this chapter.

2 Recorded by Mālik, Muslim, Abū ʿUwānah, Abū Dāwūd, and Ibn Naṣr.

sunnah of *'ishā'*, because there are no reports mentioning them in addition to the thirteen *rak'āt*.

JĀBIR'S REPORT

Jābir Bin 'Abdillāh (ﷺ) reported:

> "Allāh's Messenger (ﷺ) led us (one night) during *Ramaḍān*, praying eight *rak'āt* and *witr*. On the following night, we gathered in the *Masjid* hoping that he will come out again (to lead the prayer). We stayed there until the morning. Then we entered (to the center of the *Masjid*) and said, 'O Messenger of Allāh! Last night we gathered in the *Masjid* hoping that you would lead us in the prayer.' To which he replied
>
> **‹Indeed I feared that it would become an obligation on you.›** " [1]

IBN 'ABBĀS'S WEAK REPORT

Commenting on the above *ḥadīth* of 'Ā'ishah, al-Ḥāfiẓ Ibn Ḥajar said:

> "As for what was recorded by Ibn Abī Shaybah, from the *ḥadīth* of Ibn 'Abbās (ﷺ), that, 'Allāh's Messenger (ﷺ) used to pray in *Ramaḍān* twenty *rak'āt* and *witr*,' it has a weak *isnād*; furthermore, it contradicts 'Ā'ishah's *ḥadīth* in the two *Ṣaḥīḥs*. And she knows better than other people about the affairs of the Prophet (ﷺ) at night." [2]

Prior to Ibn Ḥajar, al-Ḥāfiẓ az-Zayla'ī expressed a similar

---

1 Recorded by Ibn Naṣr, and at-Ṭabarānī in *al-Mu'jam uṣ-Ṣaghīr*. Its *isnād* is *ḥasan* because of the previous *ḥadīth*. In *Fatḥ ul-Bārī* and *at-Talkhīṣ*, al-Ḥāfiẓ indicated its soundness, and referenced it to Ibn Khuzaymah and Ibn Ḥibbān in their *Ṣaḥīḥs*.

2 *Fatḥ ul-Bārī* 4:205.

understanding as well [1].

In addition, this *ḥadīth* of Ibn 'Abbās (ﷺ) is very weak, as stated by as-Suyūṭī [2]. Its problem arises from Abū Shaybah Ibrāhīm Bin 'Uthmān, whose narrations are rejected, as stated by al-Ḥāfiẓ Ibn Ḥajar in *at-Taqrīb*. All narrations of this *ḥadīth* include this narrator in their *isnād* [3].

In fact, this Abū Shaybah is very weak, as Ibn Ḥajar indicated. Also, Ibn Ma'īn said, "He is not trustworthy." Al-Jawzajānī said, "He is deposed." Shu'bah considered him a liar in a story that he reported. And al-Bukhārī said, "They (the scholars of *Ḥadīth*) do not transmit his narrations." According to al-Ḥāfiẓ Ibn Kathīr:

> "When al-Bukhārī says about someone that they refuse to transmit his narrations (*sakatū 'anh*), it means that he classifies him as being in the least and worst position." [4]

Because of this, this *ḥadīth* should be regarded as being fabricated, especially since it conflicts with the preceding authentic *ḥadīth*s of 'Ā'ishah and Jābir. Al-Ḥāfiẓ uth-Thahabī included this *ḥadīth* with the *munkar*s (rejected), and Ibn Ḥajar al-Haythamī said:

---

1 *Naṣb ur-Rāyah* 2:153.

2 *Al-Ḥāwī lil-Fatāwī* 2:73.

3 Recorded by Ibn Abī Shaybah in *al-Muṣannaf*, 'Abd Bin Ḥamīd in *al-Muntakhab min al-Musnad*, aṭ-Ṭabarānī in both *al-Mu'jam ul-Kabīr* and *al-Awsaṭ*, as well as the selections from *al-Mu'jam ul-Awsaṭ* by ath-Thahabī, and the combined version of *al-Kabīr* and *al-Awsaṭ* by others.

It was also recorded by Ibn 'Adiyy in *al-Kāmil*, al-Khaṭīb in *al-Mūwḍiḥ*, and al-Bayhaqī in *as-Sunan*.

All of these reports contain in their *isnād* this person, Ibrāhīm, from al-Ḥakam, from Muqsim, from Ibn 'Abbās. Aṭ-Ṭabarānī said, "This *ḥadīth* is not reported from Ibn 'Abbās except with this *isnād*." And al-Bayhaqī said, "This is solely reported by Abū Shaybah; and he is weak (in reporting)." Al-Haythamī also said (in *al-Mujma'* 3:172) that he is weak.

4 *Ikhtiṣāru 'Ulūm il-Ḥadīth*.

> "It is extremely weak. The *imāms* (scholars of *Ḥadīth*) have been severe in criticizing and condemning one of its narrators. He narrates fabricated *ḥadīth*s, such as 'No nation was destroyed except in March,' and 'The Dooms Hour will not arise except in March.' This *ḥadīth* regarding *tarāwīḥ* is among his *munkar*s. As-Subkī has declared that the condition to accept a weak *ḥadīth* is that its weakness must not be severe. And a<u>th</u>-<u>Th</u>ahabī said, 'Anyone whom Shuʿbah considers a liar, his *ḥadīth* should not be considered at all.'" [1]

Note that al-Haythamī's citation from as-Subkī includes a brief indication that his (al-Haythamī's) opinion is that one may not pray twenty *rakʿāt.*

After citing the *ḥadīth* of Jābir Bin ʿAbdillāh, recorded by Ibn Ḥibbān, as-Suyūṭī said:

> "We conclude that praying twenty *rakʿāt* was not substantiated by his action (ﷺ). The *ḥadīth* recorded by Ibn Ḥibbān strongly supports our position of adhering to what al-Bukhārī has recorded from the *ḥadīth* of ʿĀ'ishah that he (ﷺ) did not pray, whether in *Ramaḍān* or any other month, more than eleven *rakʿāt.* It (Ibn Ḥibbān's *ḥadīth*) agrees with it in that he prayed *tarāwīḥ* eight *rakʿāt* followed by three *witr*, making a total of eleven *rakʿāt.*
>
> What supports this, as well, is that the Prophet (ﷺ) was consistent in his deeds, as he persisted in praying two *rakʿāt* after *ʿaṣr* (afternoon) despite the fact that it is a time when prayer is disapproved. Had he ever prayed twenty, he would never have stopped doing that. And had that happened, it would not be unknown to ʿĀ'ishah (R) who said what preceded." [2]

1 *Al-Fatāwī al-Kubrā* 1:195.

2 *Al-Ḥāwī lil-Fatāwī.*

This strongly indicates that he (as-Suyūṭī) adopted praying eleven *rakʿāt*, and rejected praying twenty as in the extremely weak *ḥadīth* of Ibn ʿAbbās.

Reports from ʿUmar

ʿUmar Commands the People to Pray Eleven *Rakʿāt*

ʿUmar (⁂) commanded the people to pray eleven *rakʿāt*. As-Sāʾib Bin Yazīd (⁂) said:

> "ʿUmar Bin al-Khaṭṭāb commanded Ubayy Bin Kaʿb and Tamīm ad-Dārī to lead the people in *qiyām* with eleven *rakʿāt*. The reciter would read one hundred *āyāt* (in each *rakʿah*), until we had to lean on canes because of the long standing. We would not finish except with the arrival of *fajr*." [1]

It should be noted that in his report, Ibn Isḥāq had the number as, "Thirteen *rakʿāt*". Ibn Naṣr reported it similarly in *Qiyām ul-Layl*, and added:

> "Ibn Isḥāq said, 'In this regard I have not heard anything more valid and acceptable to me than the

---

1 Recorded by Mālik in *al-Muwaṭṭaʾ* from Muḥammad Bin Yūsuf from as-Sāʾib Bin Yazīd. This *isnād* is very authentic because Muḥammad Bin Yūsuf is considered trustworthy by the scholars; and the two *Shaykh*s (al-Bukhārī and Muslim) have accepted his narrations. As-Sāʾib Bin Yazīd is a *ṣaḥābī* who performed *Ḥajj* in his youth with the Prophet (⁂).

This is also recorded by:
a) Ibn Abī Shaybah (in *al-Muṣannaf*) from Yaḥyā Bin Saʿīd al-Qaṭṭān.
b) An-Naysābūrī from Ismāʿīl Bin Umayyah, Usāmah Bin Zayd, and Muḥammad Bin Isḥāq.
c) Ibn Khuzaymah from Ismāʿīl Bin Jaʿfar al-Madanī.

All of those reported it from Muḥammad Bin Yūsuf as above.

report of as-Sāʾib; and that is because Allāh's Messenger (ﷺ) used to pray thirteen *rakʿāt* at night.'"

This number (thirteen) was only mentioned by Ibn Isḥāq. It agrees with one of the preceding reports from ʿĀʾishah (R) about the Prophet's (ﷺ) prayer at night, where she indicated that two of these *rakʿāt* were the *sunnah* of *fajr*. Ibn Isḥāq's report can be interpreted similarly, thereby agreeing with the other narrators'.

From what preceded, we realize the obvious mistake in Ibn ʿAbd ul-Barr's statement, "I do not know anyone who reported eleven *rakʿāt* except Mālik." Al-Mubārakfūrī commented on this statement, "This is an invalid misconception." [1] Also, az-Zarqānī refuted Ibn ʿAbd ul-Barr's statement by saying:

> "This statement is not correct! The narration (about ʿUmar) was reported with a different chain, from Saʿīd Bin Manṣūr, from Muḥammad Bin Yūsuf, who said, 'Eleven *rakʿāt*,' similar to what Mālik recorded." [2]

WEAKNESS OF THE TWENTY-*RAKʿĀT* REPORTS

There are various defective reports claiming that ʿUmar (ؓ) commanded the people to pray twenty or twenty three *rakʿāt* for *tarāwīḥ*. Such reports may not be used to challenge the authentic reports that he commanded eleven *rakʿāt*, as established above.

It is unfortunate that there are people who claim that:

> "The report of twenty *rakʿāt* is established with authentic *isnād* from various ways."

Those who make such claims do not usually demonstrate the

---

1 *Tuḥfat ul-Aḥwathī*.
2 The commentary on *al-Muwaṭṭaʾ*. The *isnād* of this report is extremely authentic, as was stated by as-Suyūṭī in *al-Maṣābīḥ*. This alone is sufficient to reject the statement of Ibn ʿAbd ul-Barr; how then if we add to it the other supportive reports mentioned above?

authenticity of any of these alleged ways! In the following, we present and refute the most common of those defective reports.

1. ʿAbd ur-Razzāq's Report

ʿAbd ur-Razzāq reported, with a different chain from the above authentic one, from Muḥammad Bin Yūsuf, that ʿUmar (؏) commanded the people to pray, "Twenty-one rakʿāt." This wording is incorrect for two reasons:

a) It disagrees with the preceding report, by trustworthy reporters, of eleven rakʿāt.

b) ʿAbd ur-Razzāq is the only narrator who has this wording.

Even if we assume that the narrators between him and Muḥammad Bin Yūsuf are acceptable, he himself is defective because, even though he is a trustworthy ḥāfiẓ (recorder and memorizer of Ḥadīth) and famous compiler of Ḥadīth, yet he became blind toward the end of his life, making his reporting faulty. This was mentioned by al-Ḥāfiẓ Ibn Ḥajar in at-Taqrīb. Also, the ḥāfiẓ Abū ʿAmr Ibn uṣ-Ṣalāḥ cited him as an example for those whose reports became confused at the end of their life. He said:

> "Aḥmad Bin Ḥanbal mentioned that ʿAbd ur-Razzāq became blind at the end of his life; so he was getting (uncertain) reports (from others). Thus, any reporting from him after he became blind is worthless. An-Nasāʾī said, 'The reports from him are questionable – for those who reported from him towards the end of his life.'" [1]

Ibn uṣ-Ṣalāḥ also said:

> "The ruling in regard to those who get confused in their reporting is that: reports are acceptable from narrators

---

1 *Muqaddimatu ʿUlūm il-Ḥadīth* p. 407.

> who reported from them before confusion; and they are rejected from those who narrated after confusion, or at a time that is not known whether before or after." [1]

This report of ʿAbd ur-Razzāq is of the third type; i.e., it is not known whether he reported it before or after his confusion, so it cannot be accepted. This is said with the assumption that this report is secure from problems of being odd or in conflict with other reports. How could it then be accepted with these additional problems?

2. Ibn Khuṣayfah's Report

This report (of ʿAbd ur-Razzāq) is also recorded by al-Faryābī [2] and al-Bayhaqī [3], from Yazīd Bin Khuṣayfah, from as-Sāʾib Bin Yazīd, as follows:

> "They used to stand in prayer in *Ramaḍān* during the time of ʿUmar (ﷺ) with twenty *rakʿāt*; they used to read hundreds (of *āyāt*); and they would lean on their canes during the time of ʿUthmān (ﷺ) because of the long duration of the prayer."

This report is the main evidence for those who claim that it is permissible to pray twenty *rakʿāt*. For a superficial inspection, it appears to have an authentic *isnād*. Because of this, some scholars have considered it authentic. However, it has several elements of weakness, making it defective and rejected:

a) Ibn Khuṣayfah is a trustworthy narrator; however, as indicated by *Imām* Aḥmad, his reporting is *munkar* (disapproved). Because of this, a<u>th</u>-<u>Th</u>ahabī included him in his book *al-Mīzān* [4].

---

1 *Muqaddimatu ʿŪlūm il-Ḥadīth* p. 391.

2 *Aṣ-Ṣiyām* 1:76.

3 *As-Sunan* 2:496.

4 In this book, a<u>th</u>-<u>Th</u>ahabī records the narrators criticized by the scholars of *Ḥadīth*.

Imām Aḥmad's statement indicates that Ibn Khuṣayfah sometimes reports things that are not reported by more trustworthy narrators [1]. The reports of such a narrator are rejected when they disagree with those of the more meticulous narrators, and are considered *shāth* (odd) – as is established in the studies of "*Ḥadīth* fundamentals".

The current report by Ibn Khuṣayfah is of this type. Both he and Muḥammad Bin Yūsuf reported it from as-Sāʾib Bin Yazīd. These two have differed in regard to the number, Ibn Yūsuf reporting eleven, and Ibn Khuṣayfah twenty. Ibn Yūsuf's report is more acceptable, because he is more meticulous; al-Ḥafiẓ described him as, "Trustworthy and meticulous," whereas he only said about Ibn Khuṣayfah, "Trustworthy." This difference is among the weighing factors when there is a difference in the reports, as is well known to those who are versed in this noble specialty (*ʿIlm ul-Ḥadīth*).

b) Ibn Khuṣayfah is inconsistent in the number that he reported; Ismāʿīl Bin Umayyah reported that Muḥammad Bin Yūsuf related to him a narration similar to that recorded by Mālik (which preceded). Ibn Umayyah then asked him, "Don't you mean twenty-one (rather than eleven)?" Ibn Yūsuf replied, "Ibn Khuṣayfah also heard it from as-Sāʾib Bin Yazīd." Ibn Umayyah asked, "Do you mean Yazīd Bin Khuṣayfah? But he said, 'I think that as-Sāʾib said, "Twenty-one!" ' " [2]

His statement, "Twenty-one" in this narration differs from, "Twenty" in the previous one. Ibn Khuṣayfah's saying, "I think" indicates an inconsistency in reporting the number, and that he did not memorize it properly. This alone is sufficient to reject his report – especially when we realize that it conflicts with that of one who is more reliable than himself.

c) Muḥammad Bin Yūsuf is as-Sāʾib Bin Yazīd's nephew.

---

1 See *ar-Rafʿu wat-Takmīl fil-Jarḥi wat-Taʿdīl* by Abū al-Ḥasanāt al-Laknawī p. 14-15.

2 This report has an authentic *isnād*.

> Because of this relationship, he has more knowledge and mastery of as-Sā'ib's reports than other people. Thus, the number that he reported is more acceptable than that of Ibn Khuṣayfah. This is further confirmed by the fact that it agrees with ʿĀ'ishah's earlier report that the Prophet (ﷺ) did not pray more than eleven *rakʿāt*. We would surely expect ʿUmar's action to conform with the Prophet's (ﷺ) *Sunnah*, rather than assume that it conflicted with it.

3. Ibn Abī Thubāb's Report

Ibn ʿAbd ul-Barr reported:

> "Al-Ḥārith Bin ʿAbd ur-Raḥmān reported from Ibn Abī Thubāb from as-Sā'ib Bin Yazīd, '*Qiyām* during the time of ʿUmar was twenty-three *rakʿāt*.'" [1]

The *isnād* of this report is weak because of Ibn Abī Thubāb's poor memory. Ibn Abī Ḥātim said:

> "My father said, 'Ad-Dārawardī reported rejected *ḥadīths* from him (Abū Thubāb); he is not that strong; he records *ḥadīths* (from less trusted narrators).' And Abū Zarʿah said, 'He is passable.'" [2]

That is why Mālik would not accept this reports, as is mentioned by al-Ḥāfiẓ Ibn Ḥajar [3]. Ibn Ḥajar also said, "He is truthful, but faulty." [4]

One cannot accept such a reporter's narrations, because of his likely errors, especially in the current report, which conflicts with that of a trustworthy and precise reporter, namely, Muḥammad Bin Yūsuf, who reported, "Eleven *rakʿāt*," as preceded.

Furthermore, the status of the other narrators in the *isnād* of this

1 *ʿUmdat ul-Qārī* 5:357.

2 *Al-Jarḥu wat-Taʿdīl* 1:2:80.

3 *At-Tahthīb*.

4 *At-Taqrīb*.

report is not known, because Ibn ʿAbd ul-Barr's book is not accessible for us to see the *isnād* and check the narrators.

4. Yazīd Bin Rūmān's Report

Yazīd Bin Rūmān reported:

> "The people stood in *qiyām* during the time of ʿUmar with twenty-three *rakʿāt*." [1]

In *al-Maʿrifah*, al-Bayhaqī indicated the weakness of this report by saying:

> "Yazīd Bin Rūmān did not encounter ʿUmar."

Al-Ḥāfiẓ az-Zaylaʿī agreed with this [2]. Also, an-Nawawī said, "Recorded by al-Bayhaqī, but it is *mursal* (with incomplete *isnād*), because Yazīd Bin Rūmān did not encounter ʿUmar." [3]

Similarly, al-ʿAynī indicated its weakness by saying, "Its *isnād* is *munqaṭiʿ* (disconnected)." [4]

Thus, this report is weak because of the disconnection between Yazīd Bin Rūmān and ʿUmar, and may not, therefore, be taken as evidence, especially since it conflicts with the authentic report from ʿUmar that he commanded the people to pray eleven *rakʿāt*.

5. Yaḥyā Bin Saʿīd's Report

Wakīʿ reported, from Mālik, from Yaḥyā Bin Saʿīd, that:

> "ʿUmar Bin al-Khaṭṭāb commanded a man to lead the people in prayer with twenty *rakʿāt*." [5]

---

1 Recorded by Mālik, al-Faryābī, and al-Bayhaqī (both in *as-Sunan* and *al-Maʿrifah*).

2 *Naṣb ur-Rāyah* 2:154.

3 *Al-Majmūʿ* 4:33.

4 *ʿUmdat ul-Qārī* 5:357.

5 Recorded by Ibn Abī Shaybah in *al-Muṣannaf* (2:89:2).

The *isnād* of this report is also disconnected. The great scholar al-Mubārakfūrī said:

> "An-Nīmawī said in *Āthār us-Sunan*, 'Its narrators are trustworthy; but Yaḥyā Bin Saʿīd al-Anṣārī did not encounter ʿUmar.' This is true; and this report is therefore disconnected, and may not be taken as evidence. In addition, it conflicts with what was reported with authentic *isnād* that ʿUmar (ﷺ) commanded Ubayy Bin Kaʿb and Tamīm ad-Dārī to lead the people with eleven *rakʿāt*. It also conflicts with what is confirmed from Allāh's Messenger (ﷺ) with authentic *isnād*." [1]

Ash-Shāfiʿī and at-Tirmithī's Position

At-Tirmithī indicated that the twenty-*rakʿāt*-number attributed to ʿUmar (ﷺ) and other *ṣaḥābah* is not authentic. He said, "**It has been reported** from ʿUmar (ﷺ) and other companions of the Prophet." [2] Ash-Shāfiʿī said the same in regard to the twenty *rakʿāt* attributed to ʿUmar. [3]

A common convention among *Ḥadīth* specialists, among whom ash-Shāfiʿī and at-Tirmithī are considered to be, is that saying (*ruwiya* - it was reported) is an indication of the weakness of the report. An-Nawawī said:

> "Specialized scholars of *Ḥadīth* and other branches of knowledge agree that for a weak *ḥadīth*, one may not say, 'Allāh's Messenger said, did, commanded, prohibited, or any other statement indicating certitude." Similarly, one may not say for this kind of *ḥadīth*, 'Abū Hurayrah reported, said, mentioned, spoke, related, ruled, or similar things.' Such expressions may not be

---

1 *Tuḥfat ul-Aḥwathī* 2:85.

2 *Sunan ut-Tirmithī*.

3 Reported by al-Muzanī in his *Mukhtaṣar* 1:107.

used either in reference to the *tābiʿīn* or those who came after them. In all such cases, one should say, '*Ruwiya ʿanhu* - it has been narrated from him; it has been transmitted from him; it has been related about him; we have been informed about him; it is said; it is mentioned; it is related; it is reported; it is conveyed;' or other similar expressions that indicate weakness, and that do not indicate certitude.

The scholars also say that the expressions of certitude should only be applied to *ṣaḥīḥ* and *ḥasan* reports, whereas expressions that indicate weakness should be applied to all other reports. The reason for this is that expressions of certitude imply the truth of what is attributed to the pertinent persons; therefore they should not be applied except to what is true, lest the reporting person falls into lying.

This rule has been violated by the author (of *al-Muhaththab*) and the multitudes of scholars from our companions and others. Rather, it is violated by great numbers of scholars of various branches of knowledge, except the most skillful among the scholars of *Ḥadīth*. This is indeed an ugly carelessness, because you find many of those frequently saying, 'It has been reported from him,' in regard to an authentic narration. Or they say, 'He said,' or 'He narrated,' for a weak narration. This constitutes deviation from the right approach." [1]

WEAK REPORTS THAT DO NOT REINFORCE EACH OTHER

Someone may argue, "We agree that these reports are individually weak. However, don't they collectively reinforce each other?"

The answer to this questions is, "No," for the two reasons discussed in the following.

1. The diversity of these reports is apparent and not real, because

1 *Al-Majmūʿ* 1:63.

the only connected report we have is that of as-Sā'ib Bin Yazīd. The reports of Yazīd Bin Rūmān and Yaḥyā Bin Sa'īd al-Anṣārī are both disconnected; and it is likely that both of them terminate in one of the narrators from the first report. There are other possibilities as well. The existence of this possibility invalidates the chance of deriving any evidence from these reports.

2. We have established earlier that Mālik's report from Muḥammad Bin Yūsuf from as-Sā'ib of eleven *rak'āt* is the authentic one, and that whoever differs with Mālik or Muḥammad Bin Yūsuf is mistaken. Thus the reports of Ibn Khuṣayfah and Ibn Abū Thubāb are both *shāth* (odd); and it is established in the field of *Ḥadīth* that odd reports should be rejected because they are faulty; and that which is faulty may not be used for reinforcement, as is mentioned by Ibn uṣ-Ṣalāḥ:

> "If a narrator is lone in reporting a peculiar report, and if this report conflicts with reports of more precise and meticulous narrators, his report is considered odd and rejected. However, if his report does not conflict with others, but only includes information not reported by them, and if he is a just, trustworthy, and meticulous narrator, his peculiar report is then acceptable." [1]

There is no doubt that the current reports belong to the first type, because their narrators conflict with the reports of those who are better and more precise than them. Therefore, they are rejected.

It is obvious that the reason for the scholars' rejection of odd reports is their conflict with authentic reports. Thus it does not make sense to use such clearly defective reports to reinforce other reports. This establishes that odd and *munkar* reports may not be used as evidence or witnesses for other reports: their existence brings no additional knowledge.

1 *Al-Muqaddimah* p. 86.

Furthermore, it is not possible to say that the two disconnected reports of Yazīd Bin Rūmān and Yaḥyā Bin Saʿīd reinforce each other, because the condition for this is that the narrators who dropped out the rest of the *isnād* are different [1]. This condition does not hold in this case, because it is most likely that these two narrators, being both from al-Madīnah, have together reported from the same *shaykh* (teacher/narrator); and it is possible that their common *shaykh* is weak or unacceptable. Another possibility is that they received their reports from two different *shaykhs* who are both weak and unacceptable. It is further possible that their two *shaykhs* were Ibn Khuṣayfah and Ibn Abī Thubāb, both being from al-Madīnah too, and both being faulty in this report, as preceded – making Yazīd Bin Rūmān's and Yaḥyā Bin Saʿīd's reports faulty as well. All of this is possible; and the possibility causes the evidence to fall down. Ibn Taymiyyah (r) said:

> "The scholars have differed whether to accept or reject the *mursal* reports. The most correct opinion is that some of them are acceptable, others are rejected, and others are *mawqūf* (as being the words of the narrator only) ... A *mursal* report that conflicts with the reports of trustworthy narrators is rejected. And if a *mursal* report is narrated by two narrators whose *shaykhs* are different, this confirms its truth, because one would not usually expect them to make identical errors." [2]

Neglecting this important condition has led some scholars to authenticate clearly invalid narrations, such as the story of *Gharānīq* [3]!

---

1 Review *Natāʾij ul-Afkār* by aṣ-Ṣanʿānī 1:288. This condition is also discussed in depth by al-Albānī in *Naṣb ul-Majānīq*.

2 From an unprinted manuscript by al-Ḥāfiẓ Ibn ʿAbdulhādī in al-Maktabat uẓ-Ẓāhiriyyah in Damascus.

3 *Gharānīq* means idols. The story claims that Allāh (ﷻ) revealed some *āyāt* from *sūrat un-Najm* praising the idols of Quraysh and confirming the value of their

Possible Reconciliation

Some people try to reconcile between the above weak reports and the authentic report from ʿUmar. They say, "The people at the time of Umar prayed eleven *rakʿāt* at the beginning; they later prayed twenty *rakʿāt* and three *witr*."

However, since we have established the weakness of these reports from ʿUmar, there is no need to attempt such reconciliation – which should only be exercised when the reports are likely to be authentic. Rather, it is possible to dispute such a reconciliation, as al-Mubārakfūrī (r) said:

> "One might possibly say that they prayed twenty *rakʿāt* at first, and later prayed eleven. This is more adequate because it agrees with what is confirmed from the Prophet (ﷺ), whereas the first practice conflicted with it." [1]

Reports from Other Companions

There are reports from other *ṣaḥābah* indicating that they prayed twenty *rakʿāt*. However, none of these reports can withstand scholarly criticism. But since many people are deceived by them, it is important to establish their weakness and clarify their status.

Reports from ʿAlī

1. Abū al-Ḥasnā''s Report

Abū al-Ḥasnā' reported that ʿAlī (ﷺ) commanded a man to lead them in *Ramaḍān* with twenty *rakʿāt* [2].

Al-Bayhaqī said, "The *isnād* of this report is weak." Its weakness

---

intercession! This story is found in some books of *tafsīr*!

1 *Tuḥfat ul-Aḥwaṯhī* 2:76.

2 Recorded by Ibn Abī Shaybah in *al-Muṣannaf* (2:90:1) and al-Bayhaqī (2:497).

comes from Abū al-Ḥasnā', about whom ath-Thahabī said, "He is not known." And al-Ḥāfiẓ said, "He is not known (to the scholars)."

This report has another problem as well, which is the *iʿḍāl* [1] between Abū al-Ḥasnā' and ʿAlī. Al-Ḥāfiẓ said about him, "He narrates from al-Ḥakam Bin ʿUtaybah, from Ḥanash, from ʿAli in regard to *uḍḥiyah* (sacrifice)." [2] Thus in the current report, two narrators are missing between Abū al-Ḥasnā' and ʿAlī.

2. Ḥammād Bin Shuʿayb's Report

Ḥammād Bin Shuʿayb reported from ʿAṭā' Bin as-Sā'ib, from Abī ʿAbd ir-Raḥmān as-Sulamī:

> "ʿAlī (ﷺ) summoned the reciters in *Ramaḍān*, and commanded one of them to lead the people with twenty *rakʿāt*. ʿAlī would then lead them in the *witr*." [3]

This report is weak for three reasons:

a. ʿAṭā' Bin as-Sā'ib's reports became inconsistent (due to old age) – when Ḥammād Bin Shuʿayb narrated from him.

b. Ḥammād Bin Shu'ayb is very weak, as al-Bukhārī indicated, "He is questionable." And he said, "His reports are rejected." Al-Bukhārī does not make such statements except for those whose reports must be totally avoided. Thus this report may not be taken as a witness or evidence. [4]

c. Muḥammad Bin Fuḍayl, who is a trustworthy narrator, differed

---

1 Disconnection arising when two or more narrators are missing from the *isnād*.

2 *At-Tahthīb*.

3 Al-Bayhaqī 2:496.

4 Review this in *Tadrīb ur-Rāwī* by as-Suyūṭī, *Mukhtaṣaru ʿUlūm il-Ḥadīth* by Ibn Kathīr, *at-Taḥrīr* by Ibn ul-Hammām, *ar-Rafʿu wat-Takmīl* by Abū al-Ḥasanāt, *Tuḥfat ul-Aḥwathī* by al-Mubārakfūrī, etc. They all agree that this is what al-Bukhārī's means by such statements.

with Ḥammād in reporting this. Ibn Abī Shaybah narrated the same report from 'Aṭā', in an abbreviated form, saying, "'Alī led them in the *qiyām* prayer of *Ramaḍān*." This report does not have any mention of the number of *rak'āt*. Since Muḥammad Bin Fuḍayl is trustworthy, and did not report the same as Ibn Shu'ayb, the latter's report is considered weak according to the rules of *Ḥadīth* specialists.

REPORTS FROM UBAYY BIN KA'B

1. 'Abd ul-'Azīz Bin Rafī''s Report

Ibn Abī Shaybah recorded in *al-Muṣannaf* with an authentic chain that 'Abd ul-'Azīz Bin Rafī' said:

> "Ubayy Bin Ka'b led the people in al-Madīnah in the *qiyām* of *Ramaḍān* with twenty *rak'āt* followed by three *witr*."

However, the *isnād* of this report is disconnected between 'Abd ul-'Azīz Bin Rafī' and Ubayy Bin Ka'b, the time difference between their deaths being about a hundred years or more [1]. The great Indian scholar, an-Nīmawī, said, "'Abd ul-'Azīz Bin Rafī' did not meet Ubayy Bin Ka'b." Al-Mubārakfūrī reported this statement and commented:

> "What an-Nīmawī said is true. This report from Ubayy is disconnected; furthermore, it conflicts with what has been confirmed from 'Umar that he commanded Ubayy Bin Ka'b and Tamīm ad-Dārī to lead the people with eleven *rak'āt*. It also conflicts with what has been confirmed from Ubayy that he led some women at his house in the *qiyām* of *Ramaḍān* with eight *rak'āt* and *witr*."

---

1 Review for example, *Tahthīb ut-Tahthīb*.

By this he refers to what he mentioned in the previous page of his book:

> "An evidence for this opinion of Mālik, i.e., the eleven *rakʿāt*, is what is recorded by Abū Yaʿlā from the *ḥadīth* of Jābir Bin ʿAbdillāh that Ubayy Bin Kaʿb said to Allāh's Messenger (ﷺ), 'I have done something last night (of *Ramaḍān*).' He (ﷺ) said, **‹What is it, Ubayy?›** He replied, 'Some of the women in my house told me, "We cannot read *Qurʾān*, so can you lead us in the prayer?" So I led them with eight *rakʿāt* followed by *witr*.' The Prophet (ﷺ) did not say anything, which made it an approved *sunnah*. Al-Haythamī said about this report, 'Its *isnād* is *ḥasan*.' [1] "

2. Abū Jaʿfar ar-Rāzī's Report

Abū Jaʿfar ar-Rāzī reported, from ar-Rabīʿ Bin Anas, from Abī al-ʿĀliyah, from Ubayy Bin Kaʿb that ʿUmar commanded him to lead the people in the *qiyām* of *Ramaḍān*, saying, "The people fast during the day and are unable to recite (*Qurʾān*) well; so will you recite *Qurʾān* for them at night?" He replied, "O Commander of the Believers! This thing has not been done before!" ʿUmar said, "I know, but it is better." So he led them with twenty *rakʿāt*. [2]

The *isnād* of this report is weak. Abū Jaʿfar ar-Rāzī's name is ʿĪsā Bin Abī ʿĪsā Bin Māhān. Ath-Thahabī included him in his book *aḍ-Ḍuʿafāʾ* (the Weak Ones) and said, "Abū Zarʿah said, 'He makes frequent errors.' Aḥmad described him as, 'Not competent.' And once he said, 'He is passable.' Al-Fallās said, 'He is erroneous in reporting.' While someone else said, 'He is trustworthy.'"

Ath-Thahabī also included him in his book *al-Kunā* and said, "All of the scholars of *Ḥadīth* have condemned him." And Ibn ul-Qayyim said, "He is known for his *munkar* reports. None at all among the scholars of *Ḥadīth* would accept his lone reports."

---

1 It is also recorded by Ibn Naṣr.

2 Recorded by aḍ-Ḍiyāʾ ul-Maqdisī in *al-Mukhtārah* (1:384).

Any researcher in *Ḥadīth* can easily see this erroneous pattern of Abū Ja'far ar-Rāzī, because his reports frequently conflict with those of the trustworthy narrators [1].

In the current report, Abū Ja'far conflicts with the previously established authentic report of 'Umar (﷠) commanding Ubayy to lead the people with eleven *rak'āt*. One cannot imagine Ubayy departing from 'Umar's authentic command, which conforms with the *Sunnah* of the Prophet (ﷺ).

Another problem with this report is that Ubayy said, "This thing has not been done before!" One cannot imagine Ubayy saying this, nor 'Umar agreeing to it, when this was a practice of the Prophet (ﷺ) that both of them must have witnesses or known.

REPORT FROM IBN MAS'ŪD

Zayd Bin Wahab (r) reported, "'Abdullāh Bin Mas'ūd would lead us in the prayer during *Ramaḍān*, finishing the prayer while there was still some part of the night." Al-A'mash [2] added, "He prayed twenty *rak'āt* and three *witr*." [3]

Al-Mubārakfūrī commented on this report, "This is also disconnected, because al-A'mash did not encounter Ibn Mas'ūd." [4]

Al-Mubārakfūrī's statement is correct, for, even though the *isnād* of this report is authentic up to al-A'mash [5], there are either one or

---

[1] Another example is his report that, "The Prophet (ﷺ) continued to make *qunūt* in *fajr* prayers until he departed from this life." This conflicts with Anas's (﷠) authentic report that, "The Prophet (ﷺ) would not make *qunūt* except when supplicating for some people or cursing some people."

[2] His name is Sulaymān Bin Mahrān. He was one of the great scholars of *Ḥadīth* and other branches of knowledge. He died in 147H.

[3] Recorded by Ibn Naṣr al-Marwazī in *Qiyām ul-Layl* (p. 91). This is a very valuable book, whose author has recorded many reports that are hard to find in other compilations. This book was abbreviated by al-Maqrīzī, who dropped off the *isnād*s of many of the reports (including the current one), reducing its value, and making it hard to judge such reports. The book was printed in India.

[4] *Tuḥfat ul-Aḥwathī* 2:75.

[5] Al-'Aynī included the *isnād* of this report, from Ibn Naṣr, in *'Umdat ul-Aḥkām*

two narrators missing between him and Ibn Masʿūd.

What Was the Consensus of the Companions?

From the above discussion, it is clear that the *ṣaḥābah* (ﷺ) did not pray twenty *rakʿāt* for *tarāwīḥ*. Thus, there is no basis for the claim that, "The *ṣaḥābah* had a consensus that *tarāwīḥ* should be twenty *rakʿāt*." [1] Because of this, the great scholar al-Mubārakfūrī stated, "These claims are invalid." [2]

Similarly, there is no basis for the claim that, "There are *mutawātir* [3] reports that the *ṣaḥābah*, the *tābiʿūn*, and those who followed them until our time, have all prayed *qiyām* twenty *rakʿāt*." As established above, this is a false claim, because this number cannot be authentically attributed to any of the *ṣaḥābah*; rather, it conflicts with ʿUmar's command to pray eleven *rakʿāt*.

This should alert the scholars to be careful, and not to accept claims of *ijmāʿ* (consensus) without proper verification. Many such claims have been proven false upon examination. Ṣiddīq Ḥasan Khān said:

> "People have become extremely careless in reporting consensus. Thus, we find those who have little knowledge of the scholars' opinions presuming that what has been agreed upon in their *maṯhhab* (*fiqh* school) or country is a consensus. This is indeed a great danger. By such indifferent claims, which are not based on careful study and piety, they cause a general harm to the Muslims.
>
> As for the followers of the Four *maṯhhab*s, they consider any matter agreed upon among them to be a consensus. This is especially apparent in the later

(5:357).

1 As, for example, in *ʿUmdat ul-Aḥkām* (5:357), *Mirqāt ul-Mafātīḥ* (2:175), etc.

2 *Tuḥfat ul-Aḥwaṯhī* 2:76.

3 Reports having numerous authentic *isnāds*.

scholars among them, such as an-Nawawī in his explanation of *Ṣaḥīḥ Muslim.*

This is not the type of *ijmāʿ* taken by the scholars as an evidence. The best generations: the first one (the *ṣaḥābah*), then the next, then the next, existed before the appearance of *mat͟hhab*s. Also, during the time of each one of the Four *Imāms*, there were countless scholars doing *ijtihād* [1]. This continued in the succeeding generations. All of this is apparent for any fair and knowledgeable person. But it is unfortunate that fairness is a mighty barrier, which is not surmounted except by those for whom Allāh (ﷻ) has opened the gates to the truth. Ash-Shawkānī said in '*Wabal ul-Ghamām, Ḥāshiyatu Shifāʾ il-Awām*':

'Matters of consensus reported in the books arise from situations where the reporter was not aware of the difference in regard to a specific matter. Being unaware does not necessitate that a difference did not exist. The best that could be said is that he assumed that there was a consensus. And a person's presumption is not sufficient as a basis or proof of consensus. Those who take the consensus as an evidence would not take such a presumption, coming from just a single member of this *Ummah*. Allāh (ﷻ) does not require this from His creatures. If a scholar says that he does not know any evidence from the *Qurʾān* or the *Sunnah* regarding a particular issue, his statement is not taken by any learned scholar as an evidence. If you understand this, it becomes easy for you to judge this kind of report about consensus.'" [2]

Also, the *imām* Abū Muḥammad Bin Ḥazm has discussed this issue in depth in his valuable book, "*Iḥkām ul-Aḥkām fī Uṣūl il-Aḥkām*",

1 Derivation of rules from the available evidence.

2 *As-Sirāj ul-Wahhāj, min Kashfi Maṭālibi Ṣaḥīḥi Muslim Bin al-Ḥajjāj* 1:3.

which is printed in eight volumes. One who likes to investigate claims of various issues of *ijmā'* should refer to it, because it is one of the best books of *fiqh* fundamentals, based on correct evidence from the Book and the *Sunnah.*

The Maximum Permissible Number

The *Sunnah* of the Prophet and His Companions

We have established that the Prophet (ﷺ) and his companions (ﷺ) prayed eleven *rak'āt* in *qiyām*. This is the correct number that they have been reported to pray, without exceeding it, during *Ramaḍān* and at other times of the year.

There is no authentic report confirming that any of the *ṣaḥābah* prayed twenty *rak'āt* for *tarāwīḥ.* Rather, it is confirmed that 'Umar (ﷺ) commanded the people to pray eleven *rak'āt*, which conforms with the authentically reported practice of the Prophet (ﷺ). Therefore, it is obligatory to adhere to this number, without adding to it, following his (ﷺ) command:

> **‹... Those of you who will live after me will see considerable difference. So adhere to my *Sunnah*, and the *sunnah* of the Rightly Guided Successors; hold fast to it, bite on to it with your teeth, and beware of novel matters (in the *Dīn*), because every novel matter is a *bid'ah* (innovation), and every *bid'ah* is an act of misguidance.›** [1]

To this last statement, he (ﷺ) added in another *ḥadīth*:

> **‹And every act of misguidance is in the fire.›** [2]

---

1 Recorded by Aḥmad, Abū Dāwūd, at-Tirmithī, Ibn Mājah, and al-Ḥākim, with various chains from al-'Irbāḍ Bin Sāriyah (ﷺ). It was judged to be authentic by at-Tirmithī, al-Ḥākim, ath-Thahabī, and others; and we concur with their judgement.

2 Recorded by an-Nasā'ī, Abū Nu'aym (in *al-Ḥulyah*), and al-Bayhaqī (in *al-Asmā'u*

It is well known that the scholars have differed in many matters of *fiqh*, among which is this issue of the number of *rakʿāt* for *tarāwīḥ*. We find in this regard eight different opinions:

> "Forty-one, thirty-six, thirty-four, twenty-eight, twenty-four, twenty, sixteen, and eleven *rakʿāt*." [1]

The above *ḥadīth* indicates the way to resolve any difference that appears among Muslims. Since this matter is something in which the people have differed, we should resolve it by referring to the *Sunnah* of the Prophet (ﷺ), which is nothing but to pray eleven *rakʿāt*. It is indeed an obligation to follow this, and drop anything that differs with it – especially since the *sunnah* of the Rightly Guided Successors (*Khulafā̕*) conforms with it as well.

Had additional *rakʿāt*, over the authentically reported eleven, been confirmed from any of the Rightly Guided Successors or others among the knowledgeable companions, we would then have conceded to their being permissible. The reason for this is that we trust their knowledge and virtue, their rejection of innovations in *Dīn*, and their great concern to forbid people from innovating.

However, since none of this was confirmed from them, as has been established above, we do not consider the addition permissible.

This, we hope, should provide a reminder for those who claim that they love the *ṣaḥābah* and desire to defend their teachings. A true defender of the *ṣaḥābah* would verify the reports from them, and then abide by them.

Is "More" Always Good?

We believe that adding to the correct number of *tarāwīḥ* conflicts with the *Sunnah*, because the acts of worship must be restricted to teachings of the *Qurʾān* and *Sunnah*, without allowing one to supplement or alter

---

waṣ-Ṣifāt), with an authentic *isnād* from Jābir Bin ʿAbdillāh. Note that some people mistakenly consider this as part of the previous *ḥadīth* of al-ʿIrbāḍ.

1 Al-ʿAynī reported these opinions (5:356-357), and then mentioned that the last number is that chosen by Imām Mālik, as well as Abū Bakr Bin al-ʿArabī.

them based on conjecture and innovation.

One should realize that in many cases, "Too much is as bad as too little." An interesting narration that would be relevant in this regard is reported from Mujāhid, who said:

> "A man came to Ibn ʿAbbās and said, 'I was traveling with one of my friends; I performed my prayer complete, and my friend made *qaṣr* (shortening the prayer).' Ibn ʿAbbās responded, 'Rather, it is you whose prayer was short, whereas your friend's prayer was complete!'" [1]

This shows the great understanding of Ibn ʿAbbās, when he indicated that the actual perfection and completion is in following the *Sunnah* of the Prophet (ﷺ), and true deficiency and inconsistency is in anything that differs with it, even if it were larger in number. This is not surprising from him, because Allāh's Messenger (ﷺ) made *duʿāʾ* for him by saying:

> **‹O Allāh! Give him the understanding of *Dīn*, and teach him the knowledge of *Qurʾān*.›** [2]

Indeed, a person with a true understanding cannot go beyond these words of Ibn ʿAbbās, but rather accept them as the rule in regard to everything in *Islām*. Anything contrary to this would lead to attributing incompleteness and imperfection to the Wise Legislator (Allāh); and verily:

(وَمَا كَانَ رَبُّكَ نَسِيًّا) مريم ٦٤

«Your Lord is never forgetful.» [3]

In his debate with the Shiite Ibn ul-Muṭahhar, Ibn Taymiyyah said:

---

1 Recorded by Ibn Abī Shaybah in *al-Muṣannaf* (2:110:2).

2 Al-Bukhārī and others.

3 *Maryam* 19:64.

"You claim that ʿAlī used to pray one thousand *rakʿāt* every day and night. This is not true. Our Prophet (ﷺ) would not pray at night more than thirteen *rakʿāt*. Also, it is not recommended to pray all night; rather it is disliked, because the Prophet (ﷺ) said to ʿAmr Bin al-ʿĀṣ, **‹Your body has a right on you.›**

Furthermore, the Prophet (ﷺ) used to pray about forty *rakʿāt* during the day and night. ʿAlī's knowledge of the Prophet's (ﷺ) *Sunnah*, and his great concern to adhere to it, would not allow him to deviate from it – assuming that such a deviation is possible.

However, it is impossible to pray one thousand *rakʿāt* and still perform all his other obligations; he has obligations toward himself: the needs of sleep, food, drink, toilet, *wuḍūʾ*, approaching his wives, looking after his family and subjects, etc., all of which would fill half of his time.

In the remaining half, he should pray about eighty *rakʿāt* per hour. One cannot pray eighty *rakʿāt* in one hour unless it is by reading the *Fātiḥah* only, and without serenity. ʿAlī (ؓ) is much better than to pray a prayer like that of the hypocrites, which is similar to the pecking of birds, and in which they seldom remember Allāh – as is reported in the two *Ṣaḥīḥs*." [1]

Note how Ibn Taymiyyah elevates ʿAlī (ؓ) above possibly adding to the *Sunnah* of the Prophet (ﷺ) by saying, "ʿAlī's knowledge of the Prophet's (ﷺ) *Sunnah*, and his great concern to adhere to it, would not allow him to deviate from it."

Regulated *Nafl* Prayers

For *nafl* prayers, such as the regular *sunnah*, the *istisqāʾ* (asking for rain), and the *kusūf* (eclipse) prayers, the Prophet (ﷺ) maintained a definite number of *rakʿāt*.

1 *Al-Muntaqā min Minhāj il-Iʿtidāl* p. 169-170.

This practice is regarded by the scholars as a confirmed evidence that one may not exceed these numbers. For example, under the chapter of "The two *rakʿāt* before *ẓuhr* (noon)", al-Bukhārī recorded the *ḥadīth* narrated by Ibn ʿUmar that:

> "The Prophet (ﷺ) prayed two *rakʿāt* before *ẓuhr*."

He followed this with the *ḥadīth* of ʿĀ'ishah (R) that:

> "The Prophet (ﷺ) did not neglect praying four *rakʿāt* before *ẓuhr*." [1]

In *Fatḥ ul-Bārī*, al-Ḥāfẓ explained that al-Bukhārī implied that these two *rakʿāt* before *ẓuhr* are not a fixed limit that may not be exceeded. Al-Ḥāfẓ's statement clearly indicates that he believed that one may not exceed (without a clear evidence) the number of *rakʿāt* set by the Prophet (ﷺ).

Likewise, one may not exceed the reported number of *rakʿāt* in *tarāwīḥ*. Anyone who claims contrary to this needs to provide evidence for his claim; and that is not possible!

Tarāwīḥ prayer is not an unrestricted *nafl* prayer, and one may not pray it with any number that he chooses. Rather, it is a confirmed regulated *sunnah* prayer. The scholar Ibn Ḥajar al-Haythamī said:

> "The difference between unrestricted *nafl* prayers and other prayers is that the earlier are not fixed with a specific number, leaving it open for the worshipper to do as much of them as he chooses." [2]

Since *tarāwī* has been fixed with a specific number (of eleven) that

---

1 According to the *Shāfiʿīs*, the correct *sunnah* before *ẓuhr* is two *rakʿāt*. According to the *Ḥanafīs*, it is four. Since both of these numbers are confirmed from the Prophet (ﷺ), reconciliation between them may be done by saying that the minimum *sunnah* prayer is two, and that the four, which he (ﷺ) was not consistent in praying, are recommended.

2 *Al-Fatāwī al-Kubrā* 1:193.

the Prophet (ﷺ) never exceeded, it is therefore a restricted *nafl* prayer, and one does not have the option to increase. According to an-Nawawī:

> "*Tarāwīḥ* resembles the obligatory prayers in that it is permitted to pray it in *jamāʿah*. Thus, it may not be changed from the way it has been established." [1]

THE MEANING OF *BIDʿAH*

Even if we admit that *tarāwīḥ* is an unrestricted *nafl* prayer, we would not be allowed to restrict it to a specific number (like twenty), because it is not permissible to adhere in acts of worship to a specific habit that was not practiced by the Prophet (ﷺ). Mullā Aḥmad ar-Rūmī said:

> "If a practice was not adopted (by the Prophet ﷺ and his companions) during the First Generation, that means one of the following:
>
> 1) There was no need for it.
> 2) Something prevented them from performing it.
> 3) They were unaware of its importance.
> 4) They were lazy or did not have the desire to perform it.
> 5) It was not permissible.
>
> The first two possibilities do not hold in the case of purely bodily worships, because the need to come closer to Allāh (ﷻ) never stops; and after *Islām* gained power, there was nothing to prevent performing them. Also, one cannot expect that the Prophet (ﷺ) was unaware or lazy in performing an act of worship. This is one of the worst thoughts, which leads to *kufr* (disbelief). Thus the only remaining possibility is that such a practice is wrong and impermissible.

1 Reported from an-Nawawī by al-Qasṭalānī in *Sharḥ ul-Bukhārī* (3:4) and al-Haythamī in *al-Fatāwī* (1:193).

A similar thing can be said regarding acts of worships that were not practiced by the *ṣaḥābah*.

If an innovated practice were to be considered a good *bidʿah* for the mere reason that it is an act of worship, there would not then exist any bad *bidʿah*s in worship! Furthermore, in that case, there would be no reason for the scholars to warn people from various innovated acts of worship, such as the *Raghāʾib* prayer, singing during the *khutbah*, *a͟thān*, and *Qurʾān*ic recitation, making loud *͟thikr* while walking with the funeral, etc.

Anyone who claims that such practices are good should be told that the good acts are only those whose goodness has been confirmed with proofs from the *sharʿ* – and therefore they would not count as *bidʿah*s."[1]

In this regard also, ʿAbdullāh Bin ʿUmar (ﷺ) said:

"Every *bidʿah* is an act of misguidance, even if the people see it good."

Some Scholarly Statements

A number of great scholars have held the position that it is not permissible to pray more than eleven. Among them is Imām Mālik (in one of the two reports from him). As-Suyūṭī said:

"Al-Jūrī [2], one of our companions, reported that Mālik said, 'The number of *rakʿāt* upon which ʿUmar Bin al-Khaṭṭāb gathered the people is more beloved to me – which is eleven *rakʿāt*. It is also the prayer of Allāh's Messenger (ﷺ).' He was asked, 'Eleven *rakʿāt*

1 Reported by ʿAlī Maḥfūẓ in *al-Ibdāʿ fī Maḍārr il-Ibtidāʿ* (p. 21-22).

2 There's a number of *Shāfiʿī* scholars who have this surname. It is not clear which one of them as-Suyūṭī meant here.

> including *witr*?' He replied, 'Yes; and thirteen *rakʿāt* are close to that (in correctness) [1].' He then added, 'And I do not understand from where people have innovated this many *rakʿāt*.'" [2]

Imām Ibn ul-ʿArabī mentioned the conflicting reports from ʿUmar, and the opinion that there is no fixed number for the *rakʿāt* of *tarāwīḥ*. He then said:

> "The correct position is to pray eleven *rakʿāt*, which is the way the Prophet (ﷺ) prayed his *qiyām*. All other numbers have no basis or proof. If we were to set a limit, let it be the number that the Prophet (ﷺ) prayed. He (ﷺ) never prayed in *Ramaḍān* or in other months more than eleven *rakʿāt*. This prayer is the *qiyām;* and one must imitate the Prophet (ﷺ) in praying it." [3]

Imām Muḥammad Bin Ismāʿīl aṣ-Ṣanʿānī declared that the number twenty in *tarāwīḥ* is a *bidʿah*. He then said:

> "And there is nothing praiseworthy in a *bidʿah*; rather, every *bidʿah* is an act of deviation." [4]

Clarifying Some Doubts

Doubts are sometimes cast regarding some points in the above discussion. In what follows, we present the most common of those, followed by our clarification.

---

1 He refers here to some of the authentic reports from ʿĀ'ishah that were cited earlier, which included the two *rakʿāt* of *ʿIshā'*.

2 *Al-Maṣābīḥ fī Ṣalat it-Tarāwīḥ* (*Al-Fatāwī* 2:77).

3 *Sharḥ ut-Tirmi<u>th</u>ī* (4:19).

4 *Subul us-Salām*.

1. Difference among the Scholars

As mentioned above, the scholars have differed in regard to the number of *rakʿāt* of *tarāwīḥ*. Someone might say that this difference is an indication that there is no clear text fixing the number. As-Suyūṭī expressed this doubt as follows:

> "The scholars have differed in the number (for *tarāwīḥ*). If this were confirmed from the Prophet's (ﷺ) action, there would not have been such a difference – as is the case for *witr* and the regular *sunnah* prayers." [1]

The answer to this is that the reason for differing is not always that there is no established text from the Prophet (ﷺ). Among the other sources of difference are the following:

* The authentic text did not reach the scholar, causing him to provide his *fatwā* contrary to it.
* The authentic text reached the scholar with an *isnād* that he found unacceptable.
* The scholar understood the text differently from other scholars.
* Etc. [2]

Thus, the difference is not always caused by the absence of an authentic text. As is well known, the scholars have differed about many issues in spite of the existence of authentic *ḥadīth*s in their regard.

One clear example is that of raising the hands during the prayer before and after *rukūʿ*. All the scholars agree that this is a

---

1 *Al-Ḥāwī* 1:74.

2 The various reasons that cause the scholars to differ have been discussed in detail by various *ʿulamāʾ*, including Ibn Taymiyyah, Waliyy Ullāh ad-Dahlawī, and al-Ḥamīdī.

recommended act, except the Ḥanafīs. This difference exists despite the fact that there are about twenty authentic *ḥadīth*s proving it. Some of these *ḥadīth*s are reported by some of the Rightly Guided Successors, such as 'Alī (⚔). And in one of those *ḥadīth*, Abū Ḥumayd as-Sā'idī (⚔) described the Prophet's (ﷺ) prayer in the presence of ten of the *ṣaḥābah*, and included raising the hands. When he finished, they told him, "You said the truth; this is how Allāh's Messenger (ﷺ) prayed." [1]

In a well known discussion that took place between Abū Ḥanīfah and one of the scholars of *Ḥadīth*, as is recorded in the Ḥanafī's books, Abū Ḥanīfah was asked why he does not adopt raising the hands; he replied, "Because there is no authentic *ḥadīth* from Allāh's Messenger (ﷺ) about this."

Abū Ḥanīfah would never have said this had he known the various authentic *ḥadīth*s that we described above. This is a clear proof that the difference in this issue is not caused by the absence of an authentic text, but that it did not reach the *imām* from an authentic source.

Thus, similar to the fact that the difference in this issue does not indicate the absence of an authentic text, so it is in the case of the *tarāwīḥ* prayer. In fact, earlier we established the existence of authentic texts, and it is not right to cast doubt on these texts because of the difference. Rather, our obligation is to remove the differences by referring to the authentic texts, as Allāh (ﷻ) commanded:

(فَلاَ وَرَبِّكَ لاَ يُؤْمِنُونَ حَتَّىٰ يُحَكِّمُوكَ فِيمَا شَجَرَ بَيْنَهُمْ ثُمَّ لاَ يَجِدُوا۟ فِي أَنْفُسِهِمْ حَرَجًا مِّمَّا قَضَيْتَ وَيُسَلِّمُوا۟ تَسْلِيمًا)

النســاء ٦٥

«But No! By your Lord, they can have no faith until they make you judge in all disputes between them, and find in themselves no resistance against your decisions, and accept them with full submission.» [2]

---

1   Al-Bukhārī.

2   *An-Nisā'* 4:65.

And He (ﷻ) commanded:

(فَإِن تَنَٰزَعۡتُمۡ فِي شَيۡءٖ فَرُدُّوهُ إِلَى ٱللَّهِ وَٱلرَّسُولِ إِن كُنتُمۡ تُؤۡمِنُونَ بِٱللَّهِ وَٱلۡيَوۡمِ ٱلۡأٓخِرِۚ ذَٰلِكَ خَيۡرٞ وَأَحۡسَنُ تَأۡوِيلًا)

النساء ٥٩

«If you differ in anything among yourselves, refer it to Allāh and His Messenger, if you believe in Allāh and the Last Day. That is better and more suitable for final determination.» [1]

What then is the real reason for the scholars' difference in the number of *rakʿāt* for *tarāwīḥ*? Our answer is that it is one of two possibilities, the first being more likely and common:

a. Unawareness of the authentic texts depicting the correct number. One who has this excuse is forgiven for not abiding by the text, as can be understood from the forthcoming *ḥadīth* of ʿAmr Bin al-ʿĀṣ.

b. Misunderstanding or misinterpreting the text. For example, some scholars interpreted the *ḥadīth* of ʿĀ'ishah, "He (ﷺ) would not pray more than eleven," to mean *witr* only. Of course, this is a wrong interpretation, because she said this in answer to a question, "How was the Messenger's (ﷺ) prayer in *Ramaḍān*?" Which indicates that her answer pertained to all of the night prayer, not merely *witr*. Besides, this interpretation would mean that he (ﷺ) had two night prayers, the *witr* with a maximum of eleven *rakʿāt*, and the *qiyām* with an indefinite number of *rakʿāt*! No scholar would agree to such classification.

1 *An-Nisāʾ* 4:59.

2. No Text Prohibits Adding

Some people would say, "We realize the truth of the *ḥadīth* that the Prophet (ﷺ) prayed eleven *rakʿāt* for *tarāwīḥ*. We also realize the weakness of the *ḥadīth* of twenty *rakʿāt*. But we do not see why one may not add to eleven, since the Prophet (ﷺ) did not prohibit it."

The answer to this doubt is that acts of worship may not be established without specific evidence (from the *Qurʾān* or *Sunnah*). This is a fundamental rule that is agreed upon among the scholars; and we cannot imagine a knowledgeable Muslim rejecting it.

If it were not for this rule, it would become possible for any Muslim to add, for example, as much as he wishes to the number of *rakʿāt* of *sunnah* and *farḍ* prayers, even though these numbers were established by the action of the Prophet (ﷺ). His excuse would be that the Prophet (ﷺ) did not prevent adding to them! This is an obviously invalid argument, and we find no need to discuss it in more depth.

3. Reliance on General Texts

Some people rely on general texts that encourage praying without mentioning specific numbers of *rakʿāt*. For example, they cite the Prophet's (ﷺ) instruction to Rabīʿah Bin Kaʿb (رضي الله عنه) (when he asked him to be in his company in *Jannah*):

> **‹Help me against yourself with plentiful *sujūd* (prostration).›** [1]

Or they cite Abū Hurayrah's *ḥadīth*:

> "The Prophet (ﷺ) used to encourage people to pray the *qiyām* of *Ramaḍān*."

They cite these and other similar general *ḥadīths* that indicate the recommendation to pray, without specifying a number.

This is very feeble reasoning, because general texts may be applied

1 Muslim and Abū ʿUwānah.

in their general sense only if there are no other texts to restrict them. The number of *rakʿāt* for *tarāwīḥ* has been restricted by clear texts from the Prophet (ﷺ). It is not permissible to annul this restriction, claiming that *tarāwīḥ* follows general recommendations. Anyone claiming such a thing might as well pray *ẓuhr* five *rakʿāt* for example, or make two *sujūd*s or three *rukūʿ*s in each *rakʿah*, because there are general texts describing the virtue of all these actions!

The great scholar ʿAlī Maḥfūẓ said:

> "It is wrong to follow general texts, without referring to the Messenger's clarification through his actions or abstinence. This constitutes following doubtful matters, which Allāh prohibited.
>
> If we rely on general texts, and neglect the clarification (of the Prophet), we would open by that a very wide gate of *bidʿah* that is not possible to shut, letting loose innovations in the *Dīn* without limits!
>
> For example, the Prophet (ﷺ) said, ‹**The prayer is the best subject. Anyone who can increase in it, let him do so.**› [1] If we hold to the general meaning of this *ḥadīth*, we cannot reject the ugly *bidʿah* of *ar-Raghāʾib* prayer or the prayer of *Shaʿbān* ...
>
> If one likes to give *a<u>th</u>ān* for the *ʿĪd*, *kusūf*, or *tarāwīḥ* prayers, how can we then stop him, and say that the Prophet (ﷺ) never did that throughout his life, when the response would be that *a<u>th</u>ān* is and act of *daʿwah* and *<u>th</u>ikr*, both of which are recommended in *Islām*? ...
>
> Indeed, whatever the Prophet (ﷺ) avoided, despite the need and ability to do it, then avoiding it is a *sunnah*, and doing it is a *bidʿah*." [2]

---

1 Recorded by aṭ-Ṭabarānī in *al-Awsaṭ* with a *ḥasan* chain from Abū Hurayrah.

2 *Al-Ibdāʿ* p.25.

4. Belittling the Great Scholars?

When we strongly insist on adhering to the number for *tarāwīḥ* established in the *Sunnah*, this does not mean at all that we belittle the scholars who accepted the additional numbers, or that we attribute innovation to them.

As expressed above (under Doubt-1), we do not believe that the great scholars based their opinions on desires, but on true scholarship and patient striving to reach the truth. Thus, they will be rewarded in all situations (*in shā'a 'Llāh*), as ʿAmr Bin al-ʿĀṣ reported that the Prophet (ﷺ) said:

> **‹When a *ḥākim* [1] makes a judgement with *ijtihād* [2], and arrives at the truth, he receives two rewards. And if he makes a judgement with *ijtihād*, and misses the truth, he receives a single reward.›** [3]

We cannot deny the scholars' bounty over us; they are the ones who have guided us through our pursuit of knowledge, and have taught us the importance of the Book and the *Sunnah*, and that we should value these two over any opinions that differ with them. *Imām* ash-Shāfiʿī, for example, says:

> "Muslims have a consensus that when a *sunnah* from Allāh's Messenger (ﷺ) becomes clear to a person, it is not permissible for him to leave it for anybody's opinion." [4]

Furthermore, differing with some of the scholars in this matter does not mean that we consider ourselves superior to them in knowledge

---

1 *Ḥākim* is one who has the ability and authority to make *ḥukm* (ruling or judgement) in one or more matters. This normally applies to a ruler, a judge, or a scholar.

2 *Ijtihād* means to exert *juhd* (maximum possible effort) to reach the right conclusion based on the available evidence.

3 Al-Bukhārī, Muslim, and others.

4 *Ar-Risālah*.

and understanding. That is not true, but is rather an invalid assumption.

We know with certitude that the Four *Imāms* are more knowledgeable than their students and those who came after them. Yet, their students differed with them on many issues. And this continues to happen in every succeeding generation: later scholars differing with earlier ones – as long as there continue to be knowledgeable scholars among the Muslims. When these students differed with their teachers, no one understood that they claimed to be better than them.

In fact, our position with these *imāms* is as expressed by ʿĀṣim Bin Yūsuf [1], who was told, "There are numerous issues in which you differ with Abū Ḥanīfah." He replied:

> "Abū Ḥanīfah has been given (of knowledge and understanding) that which we have not been given. His understanding reached a level that we cannot reach. As for us, our understanding cannot go beyond our level. And we cannot make a *fatwā* according to his sayings unless we understand his basis for what he said." [2]

ʿĀṣim refers here to Abū Ḥanīfah's famous statement, "It's not permissible for any one to adopt our opinion unless he knows on what we based it." So, in reality, he is adhering to Abū Ḥanīfah, even when he differs with him!

We say the above while, at the same time, we assert that Allāh's mercy is wider than to restrict knowledge and virtue to these Four *Imāms* only. Allāh (ﷻ) is indeed capable of creating after them those who are more knowledgeable in some issues. Also, a lesser person could possess knowledge that a better person does not possess. This is well recognized among the scholars; and the Prophet (ﷺ) said:

> **‹My nation is like rain; it is not possible to tell whether the goodness is in its beginning or its end.›** [3]

---

1 He was a student of the two great *imāms*, Muḥammad and Abū Yūsuf.

2 Reported by al-Fillānī in *Īqāẓ ul-Himam* (p. 51-52) from the scholar Abū al-Layth as-Samarqandī.

3 Recorded by at-Tirmi<u>th</u>ī (who verified it to be *ḥasan*), al-ʿUqaylī, and others, with

Safety in Adhering to the *Sunnah*

Regardless of what arguments are presented for or against adding to the reported number of *rakʿāt*, no Muslim should hesitate in acknowledging that the best number to pray is that confirmed from the Prophet (ﷺ), as he (ﷺ) said:

> **‹The best guidance is the guidance of Muḥammad (ﷺ).›** [1]

Nothing should prevent the Muslims today from adhering to this *sunnah*, thereby fulfilling the Prophet's (ﷺ) instruction:

> **‹Leave what gives you doubt, for that which does not give you doubt.›** [2]

This should be further emphasized when we realize that most Muslims who perform *tarāwīḥ* as twenty *rakʿāt* abuse this prayer by performing it so fast as to lose all form of *khushūʿ* (devotion) and serenity. By that, they make all of their prayer liable to being annulled and rejected. Had they only prayed the correct number confirmed in the *Sunnah*, spending the same amount of time to perform it, their prayer would be more correct and acceptable by any scholar's judgement. Jābir (رضي الله عنه) reported that the Prophet (ﷺ) said:

> **‹The best prayer is that with long *qunūt* (standing)** [3]**.›** [4]

---

various *isnāds*.

1 Muslim.

2 Recorded by Aḥmad, at-Tirmiṯẖī, and others, with an authentic *isnād*.

3 This is one of the meanings of *qunūt*. Refer to Chapter 7 for more discussion of this.

4 Muslim and others.

Praying less than Eleven *Rakʿāt*

We have thus far established that it is not permissible to pray *qiyām* with more than eleven *rakʿāt*. An important question that remains to be answered is whether it is permissible to pray less than eleven. The answer is, "Yes," as the Prophet's (ﷺ) practice and words indicate.

As for the practice, ʿAbdullāh Bin Abī Qays reported that he asked ʿĀʾishah (R), "How many (*rakʿāt*) did Allāh's Messenger (ﷺ) pray *witr*?" She replied:

> "He prayed *witr* four [1] and three (*rakʿāt*), or six and three, or ten and three; he would not pray *witr* less than seven, nor more than thirteen." [2]

This *ḥadīth* of ʿĀʾishah indicates that what was reported from her in another narration – that the Prophet (ﷺ) prayed three *rakʿāt* for *witr* – means three, preceded by four. Aṭ-Ṭaḥāwī recorded from her with an authentic *isnād* that she said, "*Witr* used to be seven (*rakʿāt*), or five, or three incomplete." Aṭ-Ṭaḥāwī commented:

> "She disliked praying *witr* three *rakʿāt* only, not preceded by others."

And as for the Prophet's (ﷺ) words, Abū Ayyūb al-Anṣārī (ﷺ) reported that the Prophet (ﷺ) said:

> **‹*Witr* is true (as a recommended act of worship). Anyone who wishes may pray five (*rakʿāt*); and anyone who wishes may pray three; and anyone who wishes may pray one.›** [3]

---

1 The first two of them were the *sunnah* prayers after *ʿIshāʾ*, or two light *rakʿāt* that the Prophet (ﷺ) performed before *qiyām*. This is also the view of al-Ḥāfiẓ Ibn Ḥajar.

2 Recorded by Abū Dāwūd, Aḥmad and others with a good chain of narrators. It is authenticated by al-Ḥāfiẓ al-ʿIrāqī in *Takhrīj ul-Iḥyāʾ*.

3 Recorded by aṭ-Ṭaḥāwī, al-Ḥākim, and others. The chain of this *ḥadīth* is authentic,

This is a clear text which permits reducing *witr* to just one *rakʿah*. The *Salaf* practiced this sometimes, as indicated by al-Ḥāfiẓ Ibn Ḥajar:

> "It is authentically reported that a number of the *ṣaḥābah* prayed one *rakʿah* for *witr*, without praying any *nafl* prior to it. It is recorded in Muḥammad Bin Naṣr's book and others, with an authentic *isnād* from as-Sāʾib Bin Yazīd, that ʿUthmān recited *Qurʾān* one night in just one *rakʿah*; and he did not pray anything else. We will also cite in the chapter of *al-Maghāzī* the report of ʿAbdullāh Bin Thatʿlabah that Saʿd prayed one *rakʿah* for *witr,* and in *al-Manāqib* the report that Muʿāwiyah prayed one *rakʿah* for *witr,* which was approved by Ibn ʿAbbās." [1]

This clearly refutes the claims of some *Ḥanafī*s that the Muslims have unanimously agreed that *witr* should be three *rakʿāt*. [2]

---

as is verified by al-Ḥākim, ath-Thahabī, Ibn Ḥibbān, and others.

1 *Fatḥ ul-Bārī.*

2 Review *Fatḥ ul-Bārī* (2:385), and *Naṣb ur-Rāyah* (2:122).

CHAPTER 6

MANNER OF PRAYING *QIYĀM* [1]

Supplication for Starting *Qiyām* [2]

There are various supplications and *thikr*s for starting the prayer reported from the Prophet (ﷺ). In particular, there are some that he used to say at the beginning of *qiyām*. It is recommended to learn at least one of them. Learning more would allow practicing the *Sunnah* in a better way by saying them at various times. In what follows we present three such reports.

1. Ibn ʿAbbās's Report

Ibn ʿAbbās (رضي الله عنه) reported that when the Prophet (ﷺ) got up for the prayer in the depth of night, he would say:

«اللَّهُمَّ لكَ الحمد أنْتَ قَيِّمُ السَّماواتِ والأرضِ ومَن فِيهِنَّ، ولَكَ الحَمْدُ أنْتَ نُورُ السَّماواتِ والأرضِ ومَن فِيهِنَّ، ولَكَ الحَمْدُ أنْتَ مَلِكُ السَّماواتِ والأرضِ ومَن فِيهِنَّ، ولَكَ الحَمْدُ، أنتَ الحقُّ، ووعدُكَ الحقُّ، ولِقاؤُكَ حَقٌّ، وقولُكَ حَقٌّ، والجَنَّةُ حقٌّ، والنَّارُ حقٌّ، والنَّبيونَ حَقٌّ، ومُحَمَّدٌ حَقٌّ، والساعَةُ حَقٌّ، اللَّهُمَّ لَكَ أسلَمْتُ، وبِكَ

1 The **first** and **last** sections of this chapter are not from the work translated from al-Albānī, but were included here for the sake of completeness. The references used for this material are mentioned in the Preface.

2 See the above footnote.

آمَنتُ، وَعَلَيْكَ تَوكَّلتُ، وإلَيْكَ أَنبتُ، وَبِكَ خَاصَمْتُ،
وَإلَيْكَ حاكَمتُ، فاغفِرْ لي ما قدَّمتُ وما أخَّرتُ، وَما
أسرَرْتُ وما أَعلَنتُ، وما أنتَ أَعلَمُ به مِنِي، أنتَ المُقدِّمُ،
وأنتَ المُؤخِّرُ، لا إلٰه إلاَّ أنتَ، ولا إلٰه غيرُكَ»

‹Allāhumma lak al-ḥamdu, anta qayyim us-samāwāti wal-Arḍi waman fīhinn, walak al-ḥamdu, anta nūr us-samāwāti wal-Arḍi waman fīhinn, walak al-ḥamdu, anta malik us-samāwāti wal-Arḍi waman fīhinn, walak al-ḥamdu, ant al-ḥaqqu, wa-waʿduk al-ḥaqqu, wa-liqāʾuka ḥaqqun, wa-qawluka ḥaqqun, wal-jannatu ḥaqqun, wan-nāru ḥaqqun, wan-nabiyyūna ḥaqqun, wa muḥammadun ḥaqqun, was-sāʿatu ḥaqq.

Allāhumma lak aslamtu, wa-bika āmantu, wa-ʿalayka tawakkaltu, wa-ilayka anabtu, wa-bika khāṣamtu, wa-ilayka ḥākamt. Faghfir lī mā qaddamtu, wa-mā akhkhartu, wa-mā asrartu, wa-mā aʿlantu, wa-mā anta aʿlamu bihī minnī. Ant al-muqaddimu, wa-ant al-muʾakhkhiru, lā ilāha illā anta, walā ilāha ghayruk –

O Allāh! All praise belongs to You; You are the Custodian of the heavens and Earth and all that is therein. And all praise belongs to You; You are the Lighter of the heavens and Earth and all that is therein. And all praise belongs to You; You are the Sovereign of the heavens and Earth and all that is therein. And all praise belongs to You; You are the Truth; Your promise is the truth; meeting You (in the hereafter) is true; Your speech is true; *Jannah* is true; the Fire is true; the prophets are true; Muḥammad is true; and the Hour (of doom) is true.

O Allāh! I submit myself to You, believe in You, rely on You, turn into You, fight for You, and arbitrate to You. So forgive what I have done in the past or will do in the future, what I hide or declare,

and what You know better than me (of what I did). You are the one who brings (some people) forward, and move (others) back. There is no (true) god except You, and there is no (true) god other than You.⟩ ¹

2. 'Ā'ISHAH'S REPORT

'Ā'ishah (R) reported that when the Prophet (ﷺ) got up at night (to pray), he would open his prayer by saying:

«اللهُمَّ رَبَّ جِبْرِيلَ وميكائِيلَ وإسرافيلَ، فَاطِرَ السَّماواتِ والأرضِ، عالِمَ الغَيْبِ والشَّهادةِ، أنتَ تحكُمُ بينَ عِبادِكَ فيما كانوا فيه يختلِفُونَ، اهْدِني لِما اختُلِفَ فيه مِنَ الحقِّ بإذْنِكَ، إنَّكَ تَهْدي مَنْ تَشاءُ إلى صِراطٍ مُسْتَقيمٍ»

⟨Allāhumma rabba jibrīla wa-mīkā'īla wa-isrāfīl, fāṭir as-samāwāti wal-arḍ, 'ālim al-ghaybi wash-shahādah, anta taḥkumu bayna 'ibādika fīmā kānū fīhi yakhtalifūn. Ihdinī lima 'khtulifa fīhi min al-ḥaqqi bi-ithnika, innaka tahdī man tashā'u ilā ṣirāṭin mustaqīm –
O Allāh, Lord of Jibrīl, Mīkā'īl, and Isrāfīl, Creator of the heavens and Earth, knower of the hidden and witnessed things, You will judge among your servants about that wherein they used to differ. Guide me to the truth in matters of difference, with your permission, You guide whomever You will to a straight path.⟩ ²

---

1 Al-Bukhārī and Muslim.
2 Muslim.

3. Abū Saʿīd's Report

Abū Saʿīd al-Khudrī (ﷺ) reported that when the Prophet (ﷺ) got up for *qiyām*, he would start the prayer by saying *Allāhu akbar*, then before reciting *Qurʾān*, he would say:

«سُبحانَكَ اللهُمَّ وبحمدِك، وتبارَكَ اسمُكَ، وتعالى جدُّكَ، وَلا إلـه غيرُكَ، لا إلـهَ إلاَّ اللَّهُ، لا إلـهَ إلاَّ اللَّهُ، لا إلـهَ إلاَّ اللَّهُ، اللَّهُ أكبرُ كبيراً، اللَّهُ أكبرُ كبيراً، اللَّه أكبرُ كبيراً، أعوذ باللَّهِ السَّميعِ العَليمِ منَ الشَّيطانِ الرَّجيمِ من همْزِهِ ونفْخِهِ ونَفْثِهِ»

‹*Subḥānak allāhumma wa-biḥamdika, wa-tabārak asmuka, wa-taʿālā jadduka, wa-lā ilāha ghayruk.*
***Lā ilāha illallāh.* (Three times)**
***Allāhu akbaru kabīrā.* (Three times)**
***Aʿūthu billāh is-samīʿ il-ʿalīmi min ash-shayṭān ir-rajīm, min hamzihi wa-nafkhihi wa-nafthih* –**
Exalted are You, my God; all praise belongs to You, hollowed is Your name; great is Your honor; and there is no (true) deity but you.
There is no (true) god except Allāh. (Three times)
Allāh is the Greatest – He is great indeed. (Three times)
I seek refuge with Allāh, the All-Hearing, All-Knowing, from the outcast Satan – from his spurring, blowing, and breathing.› [1]

1 Recorded by Abū Dāwūd and at-Tirmithī. It is verified to be authentic by al-Albānī.

Recitation During *Qiyām*

The Prophet's Practice

The Prophet (ﷺ) did not fix the length of recitation for *qiyām*. His recitation varied in length; it was sometimes short, more often long, and extremely long on some occasions. Ibn Mas'ūd (ﷺ) said:

> "I prayed with the Prophet (ﷺ) one night. He stood (in recitation) for so long that I was inclined to do something wrong."

He was asked, "What were you inclined to do?" And he replied, "I was inclined to sit down and let him pray alone." [1]

Ḥuthayfah Bin al-Yamān (ﷺ) reported:

> "I prayed with the Prophet (ﷺ) one night; he started reciting *sūrat ul-Baqarah* (2). I said to myself, 'He will make *rukū'* after one hundred *āyāt*'. But he carried on; so I thought, 'He will finish it (the *sūrah*) in two *rak'āt*.' But he carried on; so I thought, 'He will make *rukū'* when he has finished it.' But he started *sūrat un-Nisā'* (4) and recited it all; then he started *sūrat Āl-'Imrān* (3) and recited it all. He was reciting slowly; when he read an *āyah* in which there was glorification of Allāh, he glorified Him; when an *āyah* called for asking (of Allāh), he asked; when an *āyah* called for seeking refuge (with Allāh), he sought refuge. Then he made *rukū'* ..." [2]

One night when the Prophet (ﷺ) was ill, he (ﷺ) recited the seven long *sūrahs*: *al-Baqarah* (2), *Āl 'Imrān* (3), *an-Nisā'* (5), *al-Mā'idah* (4), *al-An'ām* (6), *al-A'rāf* (7), and *at-Tawbah* (8). [3]

---

1 Al-Bukhārī and Muslim.

2 Muslim and an-Nasā'ī.

3 Recorded by Abū Ya'lā and al-Ḥākim. Verified authentic by the latter, ath-Thahabī,

Also, the Prophet (ﷺ) would sometimes recite one of these *sūrahs* in each *rak'ah* [1]. He (ﷺ) would sometimes recite in one *rak'ah* the amount of *sūrat ul-Muzzammil* (73), which is twenty *āyāt* [2]; other times he would recite about fifty or more *āyāt* [3]. And he (ﷺ) said:

> **‹Whoever prays reciting one-hundred *āyāt* in one night, he will not be recorded among the heedless.›** [4]

In another narration:

> **‹Whoever prays reciting two hundred *āyāt*, he will be recorded among the devoted and sincere.›** [5]

'Umar's Practice

As established earlier, when 'Umar (رضي الله عنه) commanded Ubayy Bin Ka'b (رضي الله عنه) to lead the people in prayer during *Ramaḍān* with eleven *rak'āt*, Ubayy used to recite hundreds of *āyāt*, until those behind him would lean on their staffs because of the length of standing; and they would only finish with the approach of *fajr*. [6]

It is also confirmed that 'Umar (رضي الله عنه) summoned the reciters of *Ramaḍān* and ordered the quicker of them to recite thirty *āyāt* (in one *rak'ah*), the moderate to recite twenty-five *āyāt*, and the slower to recite twenty *āyāt*. [7]

---

and al-Albānī (in *Ṣifat uṣ-Ṣalāh*).

1 Recorded by an-Nasā'ī and Abū Dāwūd. Verified authentic by al-Albānī (in *Ṣifat uṣ-Ṣalāh*).

2 Recorded by Aḥmad and Abū Dāwūd. Verified authentic by al-Albānī (in *Ṣifat uṣ-Ṣalāh*).

3 Al-Bukhārī and Abū Dāwūd.

4 Recorded by ad-Dārimī and al-Ḥākim. Verified authentic by the latter, a<u>th-Th</u>ahabī, and al-Albānī (in *Ṣifat uṣ-Ṣalāh*).

5 Recorded by ad-Dārimī and al-Ḥākim. Verified authentic by the latter, a<u>th-Th</u>ahabī, and al-Albānī (in *Ṣifat uṣ-Ṣalāh*).

6 Recorded by Mālik, and discussed earlier in the book.

7 This *ḥadīth*, recorded by 'Abd ur-Razzāq and al-Bayhaqī, was discussed earlier as

CORRECT LENGTH OF RECITATION

The longer the *qiyām* prayer, the better. Thus, when one prays alone, he is encouraged to make his recitation as long as possible. The same holds true when one prays with those who do not mind a lengthy recitation. The only restriction in such cases is that one should not pray the whole night except on rare occasions. This is in accordance with the Prophet (ﷺ) who said:

> **‹The best guidance is Muḥammad's.›** [1]

On the other hand, when one prays as *imām* (leader), he should only lengthen the recitation to an extent that would not be a burden on those praying with him. Allāh's Messenger (ﷺ) said:

> **‹When one of you leads the people, he should shorten the prayer; among them are the young, the old, the weak, the sick, and those who have needs to fulfill. And when he stands alone, let him lengthen his prayer as he wishes.›** [2]

RECITATION IN THE THREE *RAKʿĀT* OF *WITR*

The Prophet's *Sunnah* (way) for the three *rakʿāt* of *witr* was to recite *sūrat ul-Aʿlā* (87) in the first *rakʿah*, *sūrat ul-Kāfirūn* (109) in the second, and *sūrat ul-Ikhlāṣ* (112) in the third. Sometimes he would add to the latter: *sūrat ul-Falāq* (113) and *sūrat an-Nās* (114). Once he (ﷺ) recited one hundred *āyāt* from *sūrat un-Nisāʾ* (3) in the last *rakʿah* of *witr*. [3]

---

well.

1 Muslim and an-Nasāʾī.

2 Al-Bukhārī and Muslim.

3 An-Nasāʾī and Aḥmad with an authentic chain.

The Time of *Qiyām*

The time of *qiyām* is from after *'ishā'* prayer up to *fajr* prayer. Abū Baṣrah (⌇) reported that the Prophet (⌇) said:

> ‹Indeed Allāh added a prayer for you: it is *witr* [1]; so pray it between *'ishā'* and *fajr*.› [2]

However, one should try to pray it in the later part of the night, because that is better then the earlier part, as the Prophet (⌇) said:

> ‹Whoever fears that he will not wake up in the later part of the night, let him perform *witr* in the first part of it. And whoever expects to wake up in the later part of the night, let him pray it then. Indeed the prayer at the later part of the night is witnessed (by the angels), and that is better.› [3]

If one has a choice of praying in the first part of the night with a *jamā'ah* (congregation) or the later part alone, then praying with the *jamā'ah* is better. Praying with the *jamā'ah* counts as if he prayed the whole night, as was established earlier (p. 34).

This was the practice of the companions during the time of 'Umar (⌇), as was cited earlier from the report of 'Abd ur-Raḥmān Bin 'Abd al-Qārī (p. 36). Also, Zayd Bin Wahb said:

> "'Abdullāh Bin Mas'ūd used to lead us in the month of *Ramaḍān*; and he would finish while it was still night." [4]

---

[1] *Witr* means odd numbered. As explained earlier, the night prayer as a whole is sometimes called *witr* because the total number of its *rak'āt* is odd.

[2] Recorded by Aḥmad and others. Verified to be authentic by al-Albānī in *aṣ-Ṣaḥīḥah* (no. 108) and *Irwā' ul-Ghalīl* (2:158)

[3] Muslim and others.

[4] Recorded by 'Abd ur-Razzāq with an authentic *isnād*.

As was mentioned earlier, Imām Aḥmad was asked, "Should we delay *qiyām* till the end of the night?" In response, he expressed his understanding of this and the previous report by saying, "No, the *sunnah* of the Muslims is more beloved to me." [1]

Various Ways of Performing *Qiyām*

The Prophet (ﷺ) prayed *qiyām* and *witr* in various manners. This is not recorded in most *fiqh* books – whether abbreviated or detailed. It is important to clarify this *sunnah* to people, so that its lovers will have the chance to follow it, and those who deny any of it because of ignorance will take heed. May Allāh (ﷻ) enable us to follow His Prophet (ﷺ) in the best way, and to avoid the innovations from which he warned us.

Therefore, we present in the following sections the various manners in which the Prophet (ﷺ) prayed *qiyām*, as confirmed by authentic narrations.

After Ibn Khuzaymah mentioned a number of *ḥadīth*s describing the manner of praying *qiyām*, he concluded:

> "One is permitted to pray any of the various numbers of *rakʿāt* that the Prophet (ﷺ) prayed, and in the manners that he did. No blame may be directed to the person who chooses to pray in any of these manners." [2]

Method One

PRAY THIRTEEN *RAKʿĀT* IN PAIRS, STARTING WITH A SHORT PAIR, FOLLOWED BY A VERY LONG PAIR, THEN A SHORTER PAIR, THEN A SHORTER PAIR, THEN A SHORTER PAIR, THEN A SHORTER PAIR, THEN ONE *RAKʿAH* FOR *WITR*.

There are three reports in this regard:

1 Abū Dāwūd in his *Masāʾil*.

2 *Ṣaḥīḥ Ibn Khuzaymah* 2:194.

1. Zayd Bin Khālid al-Juhanī reported:

> "One night, I decided to closely observe the way the Messenger (ﷺ) performed his night prayer.
> So he prayed two short *rakʿāt*.
> Then he prayed two extremely long *rakʿāt*.
> Then he prayed two *rakʿāt* shorter than the preceding two.
> Then he prayed two *rakʿāt* shorter than the preceding two.
> Then he prayed two *rakʿāt* shorter than the preceding two.
> Then he prayed two *rakʿāt* shorter than the preceding two.
> Then he prayed (one) *witr*.
> This made thirteen *rakʿāt*." [1]

2. Ibn ʿAbbās (رضي الله عنهما) reported:

> "I spent one night in Allāh's Messenger's (ﷺ) house when he was at Maymūnah's. After one third or one half of the night had passed, he got up. He went to a hanging waterskin and made *wuḍūʾ*; and I made *wuḍūʾ* with him. Then he stood to pray; and I stood on his left side. He moved me to his right side; then he put his hand on my head, as if to touch my ear to alert me. He prayed two short *rakʿāt*, reading in each one *Umm ul-Qurʾān* [2]; then he made *taslīm* [3]. Next, he prayed, completing eleven *rakʿāt*, including *witr*. Then he slept until Bilāl came saying, 'The prayer, O Allāh's Messenger!' So he rose up, prayed two *rakʿāt* then, (went out and) led the people in (*fajr*) " [4]

---

1 Recorded by Mālik, Muslim, Abū ʿUwānah, Abū Dāwūd, and Ibn Naṣr.

2 This is one of the names of *al-Fātiḥah* – the first chapter of the *Qurʾān*.

3 *Taslīm*: saying the *salām* to conclude the prayer.

4 Recorded by Abū Dāwūd, and from him Abū ʿUwānah in his *Ṣaḥīḥ*. The origin of this *ḥadīth* is in the two *Ṣaḥīḥs* (*al-Bukhārī* and *Muslim*). Note that Ibn ul-Qayyim missed this report in *Zād ul-Maʿād*, where he said, "Ibn ʿAbbās did not mention that the Prophet (ﷺ) started with two short *rakʿāt*, as ʿĀʾishah did, ..."

3. ʿĀʾishah (R) reported:

> "When he got up at night, Allāh's Messenger (ﷺ) would start his prayer with two short *rakʿāt*, then he prayed eight *rakʿāt*, then *witr*."

In another report, she said:

> "Allāh's Messenger (ﷺ) used to pray *ʿishāʾ*, followed by two short *rakʿāt*. He would prepare his *siwāk* and water for *wuḍūʾ*. Whenever Allāh wills to wake him up, He does; so he would rise, clean his teeth with *siwāk*, make *wuḍūʾ*, pray two *rakʿāt*, then stand praying eight *rakʿāt* and reading equally in all of them; then he would pray *witr* on the ninth *rakʿah*. When Allāh's Messenger (ﷺ) grew older, and increased in weight, he turned those eight to six *rakʿāt*, prayed *witr* on the seventh, and then prayed two *rakʿāt* while sitting, in which he read *al-Kāfirūn* (109) and *az-Zalzalah* (99)." [1]

Note that this last report from aṭ-Ṭaḥāwī clearly indicates that the total number of *rakʿāt* (after *ʿishāʾ*) is thirteen. If we interpret ʿĀʾishah's statement in the first narration, "Then *witr*," to mean three *rakʿāt*, it agrees then with the second narration, as well as the previous *ḥadīth* of Ibn ʿAbbās.

Note also that in the second report, ʿĀʾishah mentions the two short *rakʿāt* after *ʿishāʾ* without mentioning a *sunnah* of *ʿishāʾ* prior to them. This confirms what was mentioned earlier (p. 45) that these two *rakʿāt* could be the *sunnah* of *ʿishāʾ*. They could also be two special *rakʿāt* to prelude *qiyām* – and Allāh (ﷻ) knows best.

---

1 Both reports are recorded by aṭ-Ṭaḥāwī with an authentic *isnād*. The first half of the first report is also recorded by Muslim and Abū ʿUwānah. All of those have recorded it from al-Ḥasan al-Baṣrī with *ʿanʿanah* (not declaring clearly that he heard it directly, and without intermediate narrators, from the previous narrator). However, both an-Nasāʾī and Aḥmad recorded the second report from al-Ḥasan, whert he declared hearing.

METHOD TWO

PRAY THIRTEEN *RAKʿĀT*, MAKING *TASLĪM* AT THE END OF EACH PAIR OF THE FIRST EIGHT, THEN PRAYING *WITR* AS FIVE *RAKʿĀT*, WITH NO SITTING OR *TASLĪM* EXCEPT IN THE LAST ONE.

ʿĀʾishah (R) reported:

> "The Prophet (ﷺ) would go to sleep; then when he woke up, he would clean his teeth (with *siwāk*) and perform *wuḍūʾ*. He would then pray eight *rakʿāt*, sitting and making *taslīm* at the end of each pair; then he would pray *witr* as five *rakʿāt*, without sitting or making *taslīm* until the fifth. Then when the *athān* (call for prayer) was given (for *fajr*), he would rise and pray two short *rakʿāt*." [1]

This *ḥadīth* is clear in that the total number of *rakʿāt* is thirteen, in addition to the two *rakʿāt* of *fajr*. This may appear to conflict with a previously cited *ḥadīth* from ʿĀʾishah's (p. 43) stating, "Allāh's Messenger (ﷺ) did not pray more than eleven ..." However, we have resolved this above by noting that in this statement, she does not include the two short *rakʿāt* with which he (ﷺ) started the *qiyām*.

METHOD THREE

PRAY ELEVEN *RAKʿĀT*, MAKING *TASLĪM* AT THE END OF EACH PAIR, AND CONCLUDING WITH ONE *RAKʿAH* FOR *WITR*.

---

1 Recorded by Aḥmad with an authentic *isnād* conforming with the condition of al-Bukhārī and Muslim.

It is also recorded in an abbreviated form (without mentioning *taslīm* after every pair) by Muslim, Abū ʿUwānah, Abū Dāwūd, at-Tirmithī, ad-Dārimī, Ibn Naṣr, al-Bayhaqī, and Ibn Ḥazm (in *al-Muḥallā*).

Furthermore, ash-Shāfiʿī, aṭ-Ṭayālisī, and al-Ḥākim, have all recorded only the part of this *ḥadīth* about praying *witr* as five *rakʿāt*.

ʿĀ'ishah reported:

> "From the time he finished praying *ʿishā'* until *fajr*, Allāh's Messenger (ﷺ) prayed eleven *rakʿāt*, making *taslīm* at the end of each pair, and praying *witr* as one *rakʿah*. He would remain in *sujūd*, before raising his head, as long as one of you would read fifty *āyāt*. Then, after the caller finished the *a<u>th</u>ān* for *fajr*, and dawn became apparent for him (ﷺ), the caller would come (to alert him). So he would pray two short *rakʿāt*, then lie down on his right side until the caller came (to summon him) for *iqāmah* (call to start the prayer)." [1]

Note that this *ḥadīth* provides a clear evidence for lying down on the right side between the *sunnah* and *farḍ* of *fajr*. However, there are no reports that any of the *ṣaḥābah* did that in the *masjid* – Rather, some of them disliked doing it there, restricting it to the homes, as was the Prophet's (ﷺ) practice.

This method of praying *qiyām* is further confirmed by the *ḥadīth* reported by Ibn ʿUmar that a man asked Allāh's Messenger (ﷺ) about the night prayer. He (ﷺ) replied:

> **‹The night prayer is one pair by one pair. And if one of you fears the arrival of morning, (let him pray) one *rakʿah* to make his prayer odd (*witr*).›** [2]

Ibn ʿUmar (ﷺ) was then asked, "What does 'pair by pair' mean?" He replied, "Make *taslīm* at the end of every pair." [3]

---

1 Recorded by Muslim, Abū ʿUwānah, Abū Dāwūd, aṭ-Ṭaḥāwī, and Aḥmad. Muslim and Abū ʿUwānah also recorded it from Ibn ʿUmar; and Abū ʿUwānah recorded it from Ibn ʿAbbās.

2 Recorded by Mālik, al-Bukhārī, Muslim, and Abū ʿUwānah.

3 Recorded by Muslim and Abū ʿUwānah. Note that this explanation by Ibn ʿUmar was recorded by Aḥmad as being said by the Prophet (ﷺ), and included in the text of the *ḥadīth*. But one of its narrators is ʿAbd ul-ʿAzīz Bin Abī Ruwād, who is truthful in general, but sometimes makes mistakes, as is mentioned in *at-Taqrīb*. It

Ibn ʿUmar (ﷺ) behaved with this understanding, as is reported that:

> "He would make *taslīm* before the last *rakʿah* of *witr*, which enabled him to ask for anything that he might need." [1]

METHOD FOUR

PRAY ELEVEN *RAKʿĀT*, FOUR WITH ONLY ONE *TASLĪM*, THEN FOUR MORE IN THE SAME WAY, THEN THREE.

The evidence for this is a *ḥadīth* recorded by al-Bukhārī and Muslim from ʿĀ'ishah, and cited earlier (p. 43).

The apparent understanding of this *ḥadīth* is that the Prophet (ﷺ) would sit for *tashahhud* [2], without making *taslīm*, after the first pair of those four and three *rakʿāt*. This is the interpretation of an-Nawawī, as was mentioned earlier (p. 44).

METHOD FIVE

PRAY ELEVEN *RAKʿĀT*, PERFORMING THE FIRST EIGHT WITHOUT SITTING (FOR *TASHAHHUD*) EXCEPT IN THE EIGHTH, AND THEN, WITHOUT *TASLĪM*, PRAY *WITR* AS ONE *RAKʿAH* CONCLUDED WITH *TASLĪM*. THEN PRAY TWO *RAKʿĀT* WHILE SITTING.

Saʿad Bin Hishām Bin ʿĀmir reported that he came to Ibn ʿAbbās and asked him about the way the Prophet (ﷺ) performed his *witr*. Ibn ʿAbbās replied, "Shouldn't I guide you to the most knowledgeable person on Earth about Allāh's Messenger's *witr*?" He said, "Who is it?" He said, "ʿĀ'ishah; so go to her and ask her." So he went to her

---

is very possible that he mistakenly attributed this part to the Prophet (ﷺ); and Allāh (ﷻ) knows best.

1 Recorded by Mālik and al-Bukhārī.

2 The sittings in the prayer where one pronounces the *Shahādah*, prays for the Prophet (ﷺ), etc.

and said, "O Mother of the Believers! Tell me about the way Allāh's Messenger performed *witr*." She replied:

> "We used to prepare his *siwāk* and water; Allāh (ﷻ) would then wake him up whenever He wills during the night. He would brush his teeth with the *siwāk* and perform *wuḍū'*, then pray nine *rakʿāt* without sitting until the eighth, where he would mention Allāh and praise Him, say *ṣalāh* upon His Prophet (ﷺ), and supplicate to Him. He would then stand without making *taslīm*, pray the ninth *rakʿāh*, sit, mention Allāh and praise Him, say *ṣalāh* upon His Prophet (ﷺ), supplicate to Him, and make *taslīm* so loud as to make us hear it. Following that, he would pray two *rakʿāt* while sitting. This, my son, made a total of eleven *rakʿāh*.
>
> When Allāh's Prophet (ﷺ) grew older and carried more weight, he prayed *witr* as seven *rakʿāt*, and then prayed those two *rakʿāt* as he did before, making a total of nine – my son." [1]

An important observation from this *ḥadīth* is that the Prophet (ﷺ) used to say the *ṣalāh* upon himself, and that he said that in the first as well as the last *tashahhud*. Muslims should therefore follow this *sunnah* instead of some *mathhab*s which decree that it is extremely disliked to say it in the first *tashahhud*. It is well established among the scholars that no distinction may be made in the way of performing *sunnah* and *farḍ* prayers – unless there is a specific evidence. And there is none in this case.

These two *rakʿāt* following *witr* will be discussed near the end of this chapter.

METHOD SIX

PRAY NINE *RAKʿĀT*, PERFORMING THE FIRST SIX WITHOUT SITTING

1 Recorded by Muslim, Abū ʿUwānah, Abū Dāwūd, an-Nasāʾī, Ibn Naṣr, al-Bayhaqī, and Aḥmad.

(FOR *TASHAHHUD*) EXCEPT IN THE SIXTH, AND THEN, WITHOUT *TASLĪM*, PRAY *WITR* AS ONE *RAKʿAH* CONCLUDED WITH *TASLĪM*. THEN PRAY TWO *RAKʿĀT* WHILE SITTING.

The evidence for this is ʿĀ'ishah's *ḥadīth* in the previous section.

OTHER METHODS

OTHER METHODS CAN BE DEDUCED BY DECREASING THE NUMBER OF *RAKʿĀT* IN ANY OF THE PRECEDING METHODS, IN MULTIPLES OF TWO *RAKʿĀT*, DOWN TO A MINIMUM OF ONLY ONE *RAKʿAH*.

This derives from the Prophet's (ﷺ) previous saying (p. 83):

‹One may pray it as five, three, or one *rakʿah*.›

This *ḥadīth* provides a clear proof that it is permissible to pray *witr* with these three numbers, even though none of them has been reported from the Prophet's (ﷺ) action – rather, ʿĀ'ishah (R) confirms in a previously cited report (p. 83) that he (ﷺ) never prayed *witr* less than seven *rakʿāt*.

One may pray these five or three *rakʿāt*:

a) with one sitting and *taslīm*, as in the second method above,

b) sitting without *taslīm* after every pair of *rakʿāt*, as in the fourth method above (this may not be done in the case of the three *rakʿāt*, as will be explained below),

c) or make *taslīm* after every pair of *rakʿāt*, as in the third and other methods above – which is the best way.

The Last Three *Rakʿāt*

DIFFERING FROM MAGHRIB

Nothing in the Prophet's (ﷺ) practice confirms praying five or three *rakʿāt* with an intermediate sitting after every pair (as in (b) above). Yet, this can be derived from the above general texts. But this is not possible in the case of three *rakʿāt*, because the Prophet (ﷺ) forbade making them resemble the *maghrib* (sunset) prayer. Abū Hurayrah (ؓ) reported that the Prophet (ﷺ) said:

> ‹Do not pray *witr* as three *rakʿāt* resembling the *maghrib* prayer.›[1]

There are two ways to pray the three *rakʿāt* in a manner different from *maghrib*.

1. With *taslīm* between the *shafʿ* (even ones) and *witr*. This manner is preferable because it is better founded in the *Sunnah*.

2. Without any sitting between the *shafʿ* and the *witr*.

IBN NAṢR'S UNDERSTANDING

The *ḥāfiẓ* Muḥammad Bin Naṣr al-Marwazī said:

> "What we prefer for one who prays *qiyām* during *Ramaḍān* and other times is to make *taslīm* after every pair of *rakʿāt*. When he prays (the last) three *rakʿāt*, let him read al-Aʿlā (87) in the first and al-Kāfirūn (109) in the second. Let him then make *tashahhud* and *taslīm*, then stand up and pray one *rakʿah* in which he reads al-Fātiḥah, al-Ikhlāṣ (112), and the two *muʿawwithāt* (113,114) ...
>
> It is permissible to imitate the Prophet (ﷺ) in any

---

[1] Recorded by aṭ-Ṭaḥāwī, ad-Dāraquṭnī, and others, with an authentic *isnād*.

of these manners (in which he prayed *qiyām*). However, the best choice is the one we just mentioned, because when he was asked about the manner of praying *qiyām*, the Prophet (ﷺ) replied, ‹**The night prayer is two *rakʿāt* by two *rakʿāt*.**› So we choose what he chose for his *Ummah*, and at the same time permit imitating him in what he did, because no prohibition has been reported from him in this regard. " [1]

And he said:

"Our opinion is that it is permissible to act according to these various reports. The reports varied because *qiyām*, both *witr* and other *rakʿāt*, is an optional prayer. The Prophet's (ﷺ) *qiyām* and *witr* varied as we described; sometimes he prayed one way, others another. These various ways are all permissible and good.

However, we could not find a confirmed report that the Prophet (ﷺ) performed *witr* as three joint *rakʿāt*, without *taslīm* except in the last one – as we found in the case of the five, seven, and nine *rakʿāt*. The reports of his performing *witr* as three *rakʿāt* make no mention of *taslīm*. For example, ... that Ibn ʿAbbās (ﷺ) reported that, 'Allāh's Messenger (ﷺ) used to perform *witr* as three *rakʿāt*, reciting in them *al-Aʿlā*, *al-Kāfirūn*, and *Qul huwallāhu aḥad*.'

Under the same subject, there are reports from ʿImrān Bin Ḥuṣayn, ʿĀ'ishah, ʿAbd ur-Raḥmān Bin Abzā, and Anas Bin Mālik. All of these reports are vague, making it possible that the Prophet (ﷺ) made *taslīm* on the second of the three *rakʿāt* of *witr* ... " [2]

And he said:

1 *Qiyām ul-Layl* (p. 119).

2 *Qiyām ul-Layl* (p. 121).

> "And our opinion is that one may pray *witr* as one, three, five, seven, or nine. All of this is good and permissible in accordance with the reports that we have included from the Prophet (ﷺ) and his companions after him. But our choice is as we mentioned earlier.
>
> Thus if one wanted to pray *witr* as one *rakʿah* without praying anything prior to it, we would recommend for him to precede it with two or more *rakʿāt*, and then pray a single *rakʿah* for *witr*. If he did not do that, and performed *witr* as only one *rakʿah*, this is permissible. We have reported that a number among the best of Muḥammad's (ﷺ) companions did that. Even though Mālik and other scholars disliked this, the Prophet's (ﷺ) companions are more worthy of being followed." [1]

Reconciling between Two Reports

Ibn Naṣr also said:

> "Some reports that disapprove of praying *witr* as three *rakʿāt* have been attributed to the Prophet (ﷺ), his companions, and the *tābiʿīn* ..." [2]

These reports are weak, except for the portion of Abū Hurayrah's *ḥadīth* that was cited earlier in this section. This might seem to conflict with Abū Ayyūb's report (p. 83). But they can be reconciled by saying that the prohibition (in Abū Hurayrah's *ḥadīth*) applies to praying *witr* with two *tashahhud*s, which would make it resemble the *maghrib* prayer. But if one does not sit, then they would not be similar. Al-Ḥāfiẓ Ibn Ḥajar mentioned this understanding in *Fatḥ ul-Barī*, which was approved by aṣ-Ṣanʿānī in *Subul us-Salām*.

The resemblance would be even less if one separates the two *rakʿāt* from the last *rakʿah* of *witr*. Imām Aḥmad was asked, "What is your

---

1 *Qiyām ul-Layl* (p. 123).

2 *Qiyām ul-Layl* (p. 125).

position regarding *witr*, would you make *taslīm* after the two *rakʿāt*?" He replied, "Yes." He was asked, "Why?" He replied, "Because the *ḥadīths* supporting that are stronger and more authentic." On another occasion, Aḥmad (r) said:

> "One should make *taslīm* after the last two *rakʿāt*. And if one does not make *taslīm*, I hope that it would still be acceptable. But *taslīm* is more confirmed from the Prophet (ﷺ)." [1]

Concluding *Qiyām*

Qunūt

The *qiyām* is concluded with a final *rakʿah*, in which one may say the *qunūt*, before or after *rukūʿ*. This is explained in the next chapter.

What to Say at the End of *Witr*

It is recommended in the *sunnah* to say at the end of *witr*, either before or after *taslīm*:

«اللهم إني أعوذُ بِرضَاكَ مِن سَخَطِك، وبمُعَافاتِكَ مِن عقوبَتِكَ، وأعوذُ بِكَ منكَ، لا أُحصِي ثَناءً عليكَ، أنتَ كما أثنيتَ على نفسِكَ»

‹Allāhumma innī aʿū<u>th</u>ū biriḍāka min sakhaṭik, wa bi-muʿāfātika min ʿuqūbatic, wa aʿū<u>th</u>u bika mink; lā uḥṣī thanāʾan ʿalayk, anta kamā athnayta ʿalā nafsik –
O Allāh! Indeed I seek refuge in Your pleasure from Your wrath, in Your protection from Your punishment, and I seek refuge in You from You.

---

1 *Masāʾil ul-Imām Aḥmad* reported by his student Ibn Hānī.

> **None can count Your praise, You are as only You praise Yourself.›** [1]

When the Prophet (ﷺ) made *taslīm* at the end of *witr*, he would say:

«سُبحانَ الملِكِ القُدُّوس»

> **‹*Subḥāna 'l-malik il-quddūs* – Exalted is the Holy Sovereign.›**

He would repeat this three times, extending his voice, and raising it on the third time. [2]

THE TWO *RAKʿĀT* FOLLOWING *WITR*

One may pray two *rakʿāt* after *witr*. We cited earlier ʿĀ'ishah's (R) report (p. 99) that the Prophet (ﷺ) prayed them consistently. Furthermore, he recommended praying them by saying:

> **‹Indeed this journey (of life) is a struggle and burden for you; so when one of you prays *witr*, let him follow it with two *rakʿāt*. Whether he wakes up (later in the night) or not, they will be (recorded) for him.›** [3]

These two *rakʿāt* following *witr* seem to conflict with the Prophet's (ﷺ) statement:

> **‹Let your last prayer at night be *witr*.›** [4]

---

1 Abū Dāwūd; authentic as discussed in *Irwā' ul-Ghalīl*.

2 Abū Dāwūd; authentic.

3 Recorded by Ibn Khuzaymah, ad-Dāraquṭnī and others. It is proven authentic in *Silsilat ul-Aḥādīth iṣ-Ṣaḥīḥah*.

4 Al-Bukhārī, Muslim, and others.

The scholars have tried to reconcile in various ways between this *ḥadīth* and the above two reports. We find the best understanding in this regard is that of Ibn Naṣr who said that the command in the latter *ḥadīth* is, "A command of choice, not obligation."

The *sunnah* is to recite in these two *rakʿāt*: *sūrat uz-Zalzalah* (99), and *Sūrat ul-Kāfirūn* (109). [1]

Miscellaneous *Witr* Issues [2]

One *Witr* per Night

One may pray *witr* only once per night. This follows from many of the previous reports. In addition, Ṭalq Bin ʿAlī reported from his father that he heard Allāh's Messenger (ﷺ) say:

> **‹One may not pray two *witrs* in one night.›** [3]

Commenting on this *ḥadīth*, at-Tirmi<u>th</u>ī said:

> "The scholars among the Prophet's (ﷺ) companions and those who came after them have differed in regard to one who prays *witr* early in the night, then wakes up later.
>
> Some of them took the position that he should revoke his earlier *witr* by adding one *rakʿah* to it, pray as much as he wishes, then end it with *witr*, because one may not pray two *witrs* in one night. This is the opinion of Abū Isḥāq.
>
> Others took the position that he may pray as much as he wishes, without revoking his *witr*. This is the opinion of Sufyān ath-Thawrī, Mālik Bin Anas, Aḥmad,

1 Recorded by Ibn Khuzaymah with reports from ʿĀʾishah and Anas whose chains strengthen each other. See *Ṣifat uṣ-Ṣalāh*.

2 See the footnote at the beginning of this chapter.

3 Recorded by Abū Dāwūd and at-Tirmi<u>th</u>ī; verified to be authentic by al-Albānī.

and Ibn ul-Mubārak.

The latter is the correct opinion, because it has been reported with various chains that the Prophet (ﷺ) prayed after *witr*." [1]

MISSING *WITR*

There are various *ḥadīth*s allowing one who misses *witr* to make it up in the morning. For example, Abū Saʿīd (ﷺ) reported that the Prophet (ﷺ) said:

> **‹If one misses *witr* because of sleep or forgetfulness, let him pray it when he remembers or wakes up.›** [2]

And Zayd Bin Aslam reported from his father that the Prophet (ﷺ) said:

> **‹If one misses *witr* because of sleep, let him pray it in the morning.›** [3]

On the other hand, there are various *ḥadīth*s declaring that *witr* may not be prayed in the morning. For example, Ibn ʿUmar (ﷺ) reported that the Prophet (ﷺ) said:

> **‹When the dawn arrives, all night prayer and *witr* are gone. So pray *witr* before dawn.›** [4]

The best reconciliation between these *ḥadīth*s is to say that one who voluntarily misses *witr* may not make it up, contrary to him who intended to wake up but slept through the night.

---

1 *Sunan ut-Tirmithī.*

2 Recorded by Ibn Mājah and at-Tirmithī; verified to be authentic by al-Albānī.

3 Recorded by at-Tirmithī who said, "This is more authentic than the previous one," meaning Abū Saʿīd's *ḥadīth*.

4 Recorded by Abū Dāwūd and at-Tirmithī; verified to be authentic by al-Albānī.

PRAYING *WITR* ON ANIMALS

Sa'īd Bin Yasār (☬) reported that he was travelling with Ibn 'Umar. During the trip, he stayed behind for a short while, and then he rejoined him. Ibn 'Umar asked him, "Where have you been?" He replied, "I stopped to pray *witr*." He then said:

> "Shouldn't you take a good example from Allāh's Messenger? I saw Allāh's Messenger (ﷺ) pray *witr* on his animal." [1]

This indicates that a traveller may pray *witr* while sitting on a moving animal or, in our time, in automobiles, airplane, etc. In such cases, one should do his best to face the direction of the *Qiblah* at least at the beginning of the prayer.

---

1 Al-Bukhārī, Muslim, and others.

CHAPTER 7

QUNŪT [1]

Meaning of *Qunūt*

Qunūt derives from the Arabic verb *qanata*. According to Ibn Manẓūr:

> "*Qunūt* means ceasing from speech, supplication during prayer, devotion, submission, performing pure acts of obedience, and standing. Thaʿlab claims that the latter is the original meaning. According to others, it means long standing ...
>
> Abū ʿUbayd said, '*Qunūt* refers to many things, among which is standing. This is the meaning intended in *ḥadīth*s regarding *qunūt* during the prayer, because the one who performs it supplicates while standing. More clear than that is Jābir's *ḥadīth* where he asked the Prophet (ﷺ) about the best form of prayer, and he replied, **‹The one with long *qunūt*,›** meaning long standing.'
>
> The praying person is described as *qānit* (one who performs *qunūt*); and in the *ḥadīth*, **‹The example of a *mujāhid* (fighter in Allāh's way) is like that of a *qānit* and fasting person,›** meaning 'praying' ...
>
> *Qunūt* has been mentioned repeatedly in *hadīth*s. It has various meanings, such as obedience, submission, prayer, supplication, worship, standing, long standing, and ceasing from speech. It is then related to any particular one of these meanings in accordance with the context of the *ḥadīth* in which it appears.
>
> Ibn ul-Anbārī said, '*Qunūt* is four types: prayer,

---

1 For the most part, this chapter is not from the work translated from al-Albānī, but was included here for the sake of completeness. The references used for this material are mentioned in the Preface.

long standing, consistency in obedience, and silence.' And Ibn Sayyidih said, '*Qunūt* means obedience. This is the original meaning, and in according with it Allāh says, ***«Al-qānitīna wal-qānitāt.»*** [1] From this, standing in the prayer was called *qunūt*, as well as the *qunūt* in the *witr* prayer.'

Qanata for Allāh means obeyed Him ... *Qānit* means obedient; and it means one who continuously remembers Allāh; and some say that it means 'worshipper' ... It is famous in the language that *qunūt* means supplication.

The correct meaning for *qānit* is one who stands (i.e., abides) by Allāh's commands. When one supplicates while standing, he is specifically described as being *qānit* because he mentions Allāh (ﷻ) while standing on his feet.

Therefore, the correct meaning of *qunūt* is worship and supplication to Allāh (ﷻ) in the standing posture. It could also apply to other acts of obedience because, even if they did not involve actual standing on the feet, they still involve (spiritual) standing by intention." [2]

The meaning of *qunūt* that especially interests us in this chapter is: "making supplication during the prayer while in the standing posture".

Correct Reasons for *Qunūt*

True adherence to the *Sunnah* dictates following Allāh's Messenger (ﷺ) in what he did, as well as staying away from what he avoided. This is a general rule that applies to *qunūt* as well. Thus, it is not left open for the people to decide when and in which prayers they can perform *qunūt*. This is already regulated by the *Sunnah*, and recorded in the books of *Ḥadīth* – from the actions of the Prophet (ﷺ)

1 *Al-Aḥzāb* 33:35.

2 *Lisān ul-ʿArab.*

and his companions. In this section, we present the correct situations in which one may perform this *duʿāʾ*.

1. OCCURRENCE OF DISASTERS

It is ordained in the *Sunnah* to perform *qunūt* when a great hardship or disaster befalls the Muslims, such as wars, earthquakes, floods, famines, etc. The evidence for this is the *ḥadīth* of Anas (⬤):

> "The Prophet (⬤) sent seventy men, who used to be know as *al-Qurrāʾ* (the reciters), on a mission. Two branches from the tribe of Sulaym, called Riʾl and Thakwān, stopped them by the Well of Maʿūnah. They told them, 'By Allāh, we are not out to fight with you; we are only on a mission of the Prophet (⬤). Yet, they killed them. And the Prophet (⬤) made *duʿāʾ* for a full month during the morning prayer. This is how *qunūt* started, because we did not do it prior to that." [1]

The mission of those reciters was explained in another narration by Anas (⬤):

> "Some people came to the Prophet (⬤) and requested him to send men to them who could teach them *Qurʾān* and *Sunnah*. He sent to them seventy men from *al-Anṣār* (native Muslims of al-Madīnah) known as 'the reciters'. Among them was my maternal uncle Ḥarām. Those men used to recite *Qurʾān*, study, and learn during the night. During the day, they would bring water to the *Masjid*, gather firewood, sell it, and buy with that food for themselves and the poor people of the *Masjid*. So the Prophet (⬤) sent these men to them, but they attacked them and killed them before they reached their destination ..." [2]

---

1 Al-Bukhārī and Muslim.
2 Muslim.

Killing those righteous *ṣaḥābah* made the Prophet (ﷺ) very sad, as Anas reported:

> "The Prophet (ﷺ) performed *qunūt* for one month, when the reciters were killed; and I never saw Allāh's Messenger (ﷺ) more sad." [1]

An-Nawawī said:

> "The correct and well-known practice is that when a disaster occurs, such as enemies, famine, plague, drought, obvious affliction for the Muslims, and so on, they perform *qunūt* in all of the (*farḍ*) prayers." [2]

2. Important Events that Affect the Muslims

Qunūt is also ordained in extremely urgent situations where the Muslims are in dire need for Allāh (ﷻ)'s help and protection in a specific matter. Abū Hurayrah (رضي الله عنه) and Anas (رضي الله عنه) reported that the Prophet (ﷺ) made *qunūt* for one month, after *rukūʿ*, saying:

> **‹O Allāh! Save al-Walīd Bin al-Walīd.**
> **O Allāh! Save ʿAyyāsh Bin Abī Rabīʿah.**
> **O Allāh! Save the oppressed Believers.**
> **O Allāh! Tighten your grip on (the tribe of) Muḍar.**
> **O Allāh! Give them years of famine, like those of Yūsuf.›** [3]

This *ḥadīth* was also recorded by Ibn Ḥibbān, who commented:

> "This report clearly indicates that *qunūt* during the prayers is only ordained for the occurrence of an important event, such as a victory by Allāh's enemies

---

1 Al-Bukhārī and Muslim.

2 *Sharḥu Ṣaḥīḥi Muslim.*

3 Al-Bukhārī and Muslim.

against the Muslims, the oppression of an oppressor, transgression against a person, people who need supplication, Muslims who are captivates in the hands of *mushriks*, or other similar situations." [1]

Abū Hurayrah also reported:

"When the Prophet (ﷺ) wanted to make *duʿā'* for someone, or curse someone, he would perform *qunūt* after *rukūʿ*." [2]

And Abū Salamah reported that Abū Hurayrah (ؓ) said:

"By Allāh, I will pray in front of you a prayer similar to the Prophet's (ﷺ)."

In his demonstration, Abū Hurayrah performed *qunūt* during *ẓuhr*, *ʿishā'*, and *fajr* prayers, supplication for the believers, and cursing the disbelievers. [3]

3. *Qiyām* and *Witr*

This will be discussed in detail below.

Which Obligatory Prayers?

All Prayers

The first two types of *qunūt* in the previous section should be performed in the obligatory prayers. This is confirmed by some of the above reports, as well as the following report by Ibn ʿAbbās (ؓ):

1 *Ṣaḥīḥ Ibn Ḥibbān* no. 1986.

2 Al-Bukhārī, Aḥmad, and others.

3 Al-Bukhārī and Muslim.

> "Allāh's Messenger (ﷺ) performed *qunūt* consecutively for one full month, during *ẓuhr*, *ʿaṣr*, *maghrib*, *ʿishāʾ*, and *fajr*. He did it at the end of the prayer, on the last *rakʿah*, after saying *samiʿallāhu liman ḥamidah*. He cursed branches from the tribe of Sulaym: Riʿl, Thakwān, and ʿUṣayyah; and those praying behind him said *āmīn*." [1]

A Deserted *Sunnah*

From other authentic reports, some of which were cited above, the Prophet (ﷺ) did not always perform *qunūt* in all of the daily prayers. Sometimes he performed it in *ẓuhr*, *ʿishāʾ*, and *fajr*; sometimes in *maghrib* and *fajr* [2]; and sometimes in *fajr* alone. This seems to depend on the magnitude and urgency of the situation calling for this *qunūt*.

This *sunnah* has mostly disappeared from among the Muslims. Many of them never perform *qunūt* during the obligatory prayers, whether in disasters or otherwise. Others perform it consistently during the *fajr* prayer. Both of these approaches are wrong, as has been explained above, and will be discussed below for the *fajr* prayer.

At the present time, the Muslims are in continuous problems of wars, disasters, etc. But this does not warrant establishing *qunūt* on a regular basis, in all prayers.

Qunūt for exceptional events would only apply to situations where the disasters are sudden and unusual, causing saddness or anger in an exceptional manner. Under such circumstances, it is recommended to perform *qunūt* in all or some of the daily prayers – depending on the severity of the situation.

When the circumstances change, or becomes a usual matter, the Muslims should gradually or totally cease to perform *qunūt* in the obligatory prayers.

---

1 Recorded by Abū Dāwūd, Aḥmad, and others. Its *isnād* is *ḥasan*.

2 Muslim and others from al-Barāʾ (رضي الله عنه).

DURING *FAJR*?

The Prophet (ﷺ) did not making *qunūt* regularly during *fajr* or other obligatory prayers. The above reports clearly indicate that he did it for one or more one-month periods. Other reports indicate that he cursed the disbelievers in *qunūt* after the battle of Uḥud, or on other occasions, until Allāh commanded him to stop (*Āl-ʿImrān* 3:128). [1]

Thus, it is not recommended to perform *qunūt* specifically in *fajr*, nor regularly and consistently in any of the other obligatory prayers. Ibn ul-Qayyim said:

> "It is quite obvious that, had Allāh's Messenger (ﷺ) been consistent in performing *qunūt* every morning, with the *ṣaḥābah* saying *āmīn* behind him, this would have been transmitted by the whole *Ummah* – as they transmitted the information about reciting *Qur'ān* loud during it, the number of its *rakʿāt*, and its time. If they were to neglect reporting the *qunūt*, they could have neglected some of the other information as well ...
>
> His (ﷺ) practice was to perform *qunūt* specifically at the occurrence of unusual events, and to drop it otherwise." [2]

In fact, there are clear authentic reports from the *ṣaḥābah* (including Ibn ʿUmar, Ibn Masʿūd, Ibn ʿAbbās, Anas, and Abū Hurayrah) expressing that they did not perform *qunūt* during *fajr*, and others in which they declare it to be a *bidʿah*. For example, Abū Mālik al-Ashjaʿī (ؓ) reported that he asked his father:

> "O father! You have prayed behind Allāh's Messenger (ﷺ), Abū Bakr, ʿUmar, ʿUthmān, and ʿAlī. Did they perform *qunūt*?"

1 Al-Bukhārī and Muslim from Abū Hurayrah and Ibn ʿUmar (ؓ).

2 *Zād ul-Maʿād* 1:272.

And his father replied, "My son, it is an innovation!" [1]

As for the report that, "Allāh's Messenger (ﷺ) continued to perform *qunūt* during *fajr* until he departed from the world," [2] it is weak, and may not be used to refute the above authentic reports.

Before or After *Rukū*?

If one wishes to perform *qunūt*, he should do it in the last *rak'ah* of the prayer, before or after *rukū'*. Both options are permissible according to most scholars.

AFTER *RUKŪ'*

For the *qunūt* of the obligatory prayers, most reports support performing it after *rukū'*. Some of these reports have preceded. In addition, Ibn Sīrīn reported that Anas Bin Mālik was asked, "Did the Prophet (ﷺ) perform *qunūt* in *fajr*?" He replied, "Yes." He was asked, "Was it before or after *rukū'*?" He replied, "After *rukū'*, for a short while." [3]

BEFORE *RUKŪ'*

'Āṣim Bin al-Aḥwal reported that he asked Anas (☼) whether *qunūt* should be performed before or after *rukū'*. Anas replied, "Before it." He said, "But such and such person told me that you said, 'After it.'" He replied, "He is wrong. The Prophet (ﷺ) performed *qunūt* after *rukū'* for one month only ..." [4]

In another report, Anas (☼) said:

---

1 Recorded by Aḥmad, an-Nasā'ī, and others, with various authentic chains. See *Aḥkām ul-Qunūt*.

2 Recorded from Anas by Aḥmad, ad-Dāraquṭnī, and others. This report is weak because of one of the narrators in its chain, Abū Ja'far ar-Rāzī, who is considered weak by the scholars of *Ḥadīth*.

3 Al-Bukhārī and Muslim.

4 Al-Bukhārī and Muslim. The rest of this *ḥadīth* has been cited earlier in this chapter.

"*Qunūt* may be performed before or after *rukū'*." [1]

Al-Albānī reconciles between the various reports by saying that those reports that mention *qunūt* after *rukū'* refer to the *qunūt* of events and disasters (which is done in the obligatory prayers), whereas the reports that mention *qunūt* before *rukū'* refer to the other case, namely, the *qunūt* in *witr*. [2]

However, there are authentic reports recorded by Ibn Abī Shaybah [3] and aṭ-Ṭaḥāwī [4] from 'Umar, Ibn 'Abbās, and others, that they performed *qunūt* in *fajr* before *rukū'*. [5]

THE *QUNŪT* OF *WITR*

Ubayy Bin Ka'b (ﷺ) reported that:

> "Allāh's Messenger (ﷺ) used to perform *qunūt* in *witr* before *rukū'*." [6]

Ibn ul-Qayyim said:

> "Nothing is recorded from the Prophet (ﷺ) that he performed *qunūt* in *witr* except this *ḥadīth* (of Ubayy)."

In addition, there are reports from the *ṣaḥābah* concerning this. 'Alqamah reported, "Ibn Mas'ūd and other companions used to perform *qunūt* in *witr* before *rukū'*." [7]

---

1 Recorded by Ibn Mājah. Al-Ḥāfiẓ said in *Fatḥ ul-Bārī* that its *isnād* is strong.

2 *Irwā' ul-Ghalīl* 2:168.

3 *Al-Muṣannaf*, starting from no. 7012.

4 *Al-Mushkal* 1:147.

5 See 'Ar'ūr's *Aḥkām ul-Qunūt* p. 45.

6 Recorded by an-Nasā'ī, Ibn Mājah, and others. It is verified to be authentic by al-Albānī in *Irwā' ul-Ghalīl* no. 426.

7 Recorded by Ibn Abī Shaybah (no. 6911) with an authentic *isnād*. See *Aḥkām ul-Qunūt*.

CONCLUSION

From the above, we conclude that *qunūt* may be performed before or after *rukū'*. However, it is preferable to perform it after *rukū'* for the obligatory prayers and before it for *witr*.

Miscellaneous Issues

SAYING *QUNŪT* LOUDLY

It is clear from the previous reports that the *Sunnah* is to say the *qunūt* supplication aloud. This enables the believers to hear the *imām*'s supplication and share it with him. Al-Ḥāfiẓ Ibn Ḥajar said:

> "It appears to me that the wisdom behind making *qunūt* (of disasters) in the standing posture instead of *sujūd*, even though supplications are more likely to be answered in *sujūd*, is that it requires participation from those praying behind the *imām*, at least by saying *āmīn*. Because of this, the scholars agree that it should be said aloud. " [1]

SAYING *ĀMĪN*

It is recommended for those praying behind the *imām* to say *āmīn* during the *qunūt* supplication. In this regard, we have cited earlier Ibn 'Abbās's *ḥadīth* (p. 114).

RAISING THE HANDS

In one of the reports of Anas's narration, he said:

> "... I never saw Allāh's Messenger (ﷺ) as sad. So during the morning prayer, he raised his hands and

1 *Fatḥ ul-Bārī* 2:570.

cursed them ..." [1]

Al-Bayhaqī mentioned various reports, some of which are authentic, about the companions' raising their hands. An-Nawawī confirmed the authenticity of other reports from the companions mentioned by al-Bukhārī.

This applies to the *qunūt* of *witr* as well. It is confirmed that 'Umar (🙏) raised his hands in this *qunūt*. [2]

Also, it is recommended for those praying behind the *imām* to raise their hands when he does so during *qunūt*, because of the Prophet's (🙏) general instruction:

‹An *imām* has been appointed to be followed.› [3]

What to Say During the *Qunūt* of *Witr*

After finishing Qur'ānic recitation in the last *rak'ah* of *witr*, and before *rukū'*, one should sometimes supplicate with what the Prophet (🙏) taught to his grandson al-Ḥasan Bin 'Alī (🙏):

»اللهمَّ اهْدِني فيمن هَدَيْتَ، وعـافِني فيمن عـافيتَ، وتولَّني فيمن توليتَ، وباركْ لي فيما أعطيتَ، وقِني شرَّ ما قَضَيْتَ، فإنَّك تَقْضي ولا يُقْضى عليكَ، وإنه لا يَذِلُّ من واليتَ، ولا يَعِزُّ مَنْ عادَيْتَ، تباركتَ ربَّنا وتعالَيْتَ، لا مَنْجا منكَ إلاَّ إليك«

‹Allāhumma 'hdinī fīman hadayt; wa-'āfinī fīman 'āfayt; wa-tawallanī fīman tawallayt; wabāriklī fīmā

---

1 Recorded by Aḥmad, al-Bayhaqī, and others, with an authentic *isnād*. See *Aḥkām ul-Qunūt*.
2 Mentioned by al-Albānī in *Irwā' ul-Ghalīl* (2:181).
3 Al-Bukhārī.

aʿṭayt; wa-qinī sharra mā qaḍayt; fa-innaka taqḍī walā yuqḍā ʿalayk; wa-innahū lā yaḍillu man wālayt; walā yaʿizzu man ʿādayt; tabārakta rabbanā wa-taʿālayt; lā manjā minka illā ilayk –
O Allāh! Guide me with those whom You have guided; protect me with those whom You have protected; befriend me with those whom You have befriended; bless for me what You have bestowed (on me); shelter me from the evil of what You have decreed. Indeed, You decree, and none can dominate You; he whom You befriend will never be humiliated, nor will Your enemy ever be honored. Blessed are You, Our Lord, and exalted; there is no refuge from You except toward You.› [1]

One may occasionally add to this the *ṣalāh* (prayer) upon the Prophet (ﷺ). Also, during the second half of *Ramaḍān*, one may add the curse upon the *kuffār* (disbelievers), the *ṣalāh* upon the Prophet (ﷺ), and a supplication for the Muslims. This was practiced by the *imāms* during the time of ʿUmar (رضي الله عنه), as ʿAbd ur-Raḥmān Bin ʿAbd al-Qārī reported:

"And they cursed the *kuffār* in the (second) half (of *Ramaḍān*):

«اللهم قاتِل الكفَرَة ٱلَّذينَ يَصُدُّونَ عن سبيلِك، ويُكَذِّبون رُسلَكَ، ولا يُؤْمنون بوعدكَ، وخالِفْ بين كَلِمَتَهُمْ، وأَلْقِ في قُلوبهمُ الرُّعْبَ، وأَلْقِ عليهم رِجزَكَ وعذابَكَ، إلهَ الحقِّ»

ʿAllāhumma qātil 'lkafarata 'llathīna yaṣuddūna ʿan sabīlik, wayukath-thibūna rusulak, walā yuʾminūna

1 Recorded by Aḥmad, Abū Dāwūd, an-Nasāʾī, and others. It is verified to be authentic by al-Albānī in *Ṣifat uṣ-Ṣalāh*.

biwa'dik, wakhālif bayna kalimatahum, wa-'alqi 'alayhim rijzaka wa-'athābak, ilāha 'lḥaqq –
O Allāh, fight the *kāfir*s who avert people from Your way, reject Your messengers, and do not believe in Your promises. Cause them to be divided, cast terror into their hearts, and launch Your punishment and chastisement upon them. You are the God of Truth.'

Then they said the *ṣalāh* upon the Prophet (ﷺ), prayed for the *Muslims* with what they wished of good, and sought forgiveness for the believers. Following this, they said:

«اللَّهُمَّ إِيَّاكَ نَعْبُدُ، ولكَ نُصَلِّي ونَسْجُدُ، وإليكَ نسعى ونَحْفِدُ، ونرجو رَحْمَتَكَ ربَّنا، ونخافُ عذابَكَ الجدَّ، إنَّ عذابَكَ لِمَن عادَيْتَ مُلْحَقٌ»

'Allāhumma iyyaka na'bud, walaka nuṣallī wanasjud, wa-ilayka nas'ā wanaḥfid, wanarjū raḥmataka rabbanā, wanakhāfu 'athābka 'ljadd, inna 'athābaka liman 'ādayta mulḥaq –
O Allāh, it is You that we worship, to You we pray and prostrate ourselves, and unto You we run and rush. We hope in Your Mercy our Lord, and we fear Your severe chastisement - surely, Your severe chastisement is to reach those whom You hate.'

Then they said *takbīr* and went to *sujūd.*" [1]

1 Recorded by Ibn Khuzaymah; authenticated by al-Albānī (*Qiyāmu Ramaḍān*).

Innovations and Deviations

WIPING THE FACE

There are no authentic reports confirming that the Prophet (ﷺ) ever wiped his face with his hands after supplicating in general, or after *qunūt* in particular. Because of this, an-Nawawī said:

> "This is not recommended, in accordance with what al-ʿIzz Bin ʿAbd us-Salām said ... No one does this but an ignorant person." [1]

And al-Bayhaqī said:

> "As for wiping the face with the hands after concluding the supplication, I do not know that any of the *Salaf* did it." [2]

PRECEDING *QUNŪT* WITH *TAKBĪR*

There are no authentic reports supporting raising the hands with *takbīr* (saying *Allāhu Akbar*) before starting *qunūt*. Thus, doing it is an innovation that must be avoided.

EXTENDED *QUNŪT*

An innovated practice that started in the holiest *masjids* of *Islām*, and spread throughout the Muslim world, is that of making very extended *qunūt*, especially after the middle of *Ramaḍān*.

You find the *imāms* recite long supplications, repeating some meanings once and again, tiring their hands and the hands of their followers, allowing the thoughts of the followers to roam in a confused and impatient manner – waiting for the *imām* to end his stream of unrelated ideas and requests!

---

1 *Al-Majmūʿ*.

2 *As-Sunan* 1:212.

This innovation does not have a basis in the practice of the Prophet (ﷺ) or his companions, whose *qunūt* was concise and to the point, as presented in the previous section.

Moaning and Weeping

Added to the innovation of extended *qunūt*, it has also become a common practice, which the *imams* manage to theater in front of their followers, to weep and sob in a seemingly devout manner, moving many of those praying behind them to follow them into a collectively wailing crowd. It seems now as if this is a necessary requirement of leading *tarāwīḥ* – to the extent that the *imāms* compete in crying; and the common people think that the best *imām* is the one who cries the most, and causes the largest number of people to cry with him!

This is another innovation that has no foundation in the *Sunnah* or the practice of the most pious generation who ever lived.

There is nothing wrong in crying out of fear of Allāh. But the *Sunnah* gives the highest merit to those who do it when they are alone, away from the scrutiny of others. One's fear of Allāh and realization of his shortcomings could very well lead him to cry deeply, even in front of other people. But this should be the exception, not the norm.

CHAPTER 8

I'TIKĀF [1]

Definition

In the Arabic language, the abstract noun *i'tikāf* means confinement. It derives from the verb *'akafa*, which means to dwell in a particular place. From this also derives the word *ma'kūf* meaning imprisoned. [2]

In the *Islāmic shar'*, *i'tikāf* means to dwell or retreat in a *masjid* for a specific period of time, seeking by that Allāh's pleasure [3]. The person who performs *i'tikāf* is called *mu'takif* or *'ākif*.

Ruling

I'tikāf is a recommended act of worship during *Ramaḍān*, as well as other times of the year. This is confirmed by the *Qur'ān*, the *Sunnah*, the practice of the *Salaf*, and *ijmā'*. In the *Qur'ān*, Allāh (ﷻ) says:

﴿وَلَا تُبَٰشِرُوهُنَّ وَأَنتُمْ عَٰكِفُونَ فِي ٱلْمَسَٰجِدِ﴾ البقرة ١٨٧

> **«And have no contact (intercourse) with them (your wives) while you are performing *i'tikāf* in the *masjids*.»** [4]

In the *Sunnah*, a number of authentic *ḥadīths* describe the *i'tikāf* of the Prophet (ﷺ), some of which will be cited below. There are also

---

1 For the most part, this chapter is not from the work translated from al-Albānī, but was included here for the sake of completeness. The references used for this material are mentioned in the Preface.

2 From *Ḥulyat ul-Fuqahā'* by Ibn Fāris (110), *Jāmi' ul-Uṣūl* (1:337), and *al-Miṣbāḥ ul-Munīr* (2:424).

3 From *Ṭarḥ ut-Tathrīb* by Ibn ul-'Irāqī (4:166) and *al-Mufradāt* by ar-Rāghib (343).

4 *Al-Baqarah* 2:187.

numerous reports describing the *i'tikāf* of the *Salaf* ¹. For example, 'Umar (🙏) said to the Prophet (🙏), "I made a vow during *Jāhiliyyah* ² to perform *i'tikāf* for one day in *al-Masjid ul-Ḥarām* (the Sacred Mosque of Makkah)." The Prophet (🙏) said:

⟨**Fulfill your vow then.**⟩

Thus 'Umar performed *i'tikāf* for one day. ³

As for *ijmā'*, it was declare by Ibn ul-Munthir ⁴, and approved by Ibn Qudāmah ⁵.

Weak Reports

Some unauthentic reports are usually cited to further encourage people to perform *i'tikāf*. We mention them here in order to warn against using them.

1. From al-Ḥusayn Bin 'Alī (🙏) that the Prophet (🙏) said, "Whoever performs *i'tikāf* for ten days of *Ramaḍān*, it counts for him as having performed *hajj* (pilgrimage) and *'umrah* ⁶ twice." This *hadīth* is fabricated. ⁷

2. From 'Ā'ishah (R) that the Prophet (🙏) said, "Whoever performs

---

1 Many of these reports are recorded by Ibn Abī Shaybah and 'Abd ur-Razzāq in their *Muṣannaf*s.
2 *Jāhiliyyah*: The state of ignorance (*jahl*) and disbelief that was prevalent in Arabia before *Islām*.
3 Al-Bukhārī, Muslim, and Ibn Khuzaymah. Some of the reports have mentioned "night" instead of "day". Together, the various reports mean a full day and night, which is the minimum duration of *i'tikāf* as is established below.
4 In *al-Ijmā'* (47).
5 In *al-Mughnī* (3:183).
6 Partial pilgrimage performed during *hajj* and at other times of the year.
7 Recorded by al-Bayhaqī in *Shu'ab ul-Īmān*. Review *aḍ-Ḍa'īfah* (no. 518) and *Ḍa'īf ul-Jāmi'* (5451) by al-Albānī.

i'tikāf with belief, and looking forward to Allāh's reward, all his previous sins will be forgiven." This *ḥadīth* is weak. [1]

3. "Whoever performs *i'tikāf* for one day, seeking Allāh's Face, Allāh will make three trenches between him and the fire, each trench wider than the distance from east to west." This *ḥadīth* is weak. [2]

Wisdom and Manners of *I'tikāf*

Wisdom

I'tikāf is an opportunity for a Muslim to turn to Allāh (ﷻ), in one of His houses of worship, with submission and devotion, unobstructed or distracted by the worldly concerns. Ibn ul-Qayyim (r) said:

> "The righteousness and steadiness of the heart in its journey toward Allāh (ﷻ) depends on its devotion to Him; its confusion is expelled by turning fully toward Him ...
>
> Because of this, Allāh (ﷻ) has ordained *i'tikāf*. Its purpose and spirit is for the heart to turn fully and solely toward Allāh (ﷻ), living in privacy with Him, ceasing to be involved with the created things, and getting involved with Him alone instead. With this, His remembrance, love, and devotion replace the worries and thoughts of the heart, overtaking their place in it, and becoming its only concern. Then the thoughts become busy with remembering Him and contemplating on that which pleases Him and brings one closer to Him. One's pleasure is then attained by His company rather than that of the creatures, thereby preparing himself for the day of solitude in the graves, when he

1 Recorded by ad-Daylamī. Review *Ḍa'īf ul-Jāmi'* (5452) by al-Albānī.

2 Recorded by aṭ-Ṭabarānī and others. It has an obscure problem, which is detailed in *aḍ-Ḍa'īfah* (no. 5347) by al-Albānī.

> will have no company or delight except Him. This is the greatest purpose of *iʿtikāf*." [1]

And Ibn Rajab (r) said:

> "The meaning and reality of *iʿtikāf* is that one severs all ties with the created things in order to be dedicated to serving the Creator. As one's knowledge about Allāh, love for Him, and pleasure in His company increase, he gains full and complete devotion to Allāh (ﷻ) in all situations." [2]

MANNERS DURING *IʿTIKĀF*

A *muʿtakif* should not forget the great wisdom and purpose of *iʿtikāf* outlined above. He should pass the days of *iʿtikāf* in tranquility and devotion, dedicating his time to Allāh (ﷻ), and spending it in performing acts of pure worship, such as prayer, reading *Qurʾān,* making *thikr*, seeking *Islām*ic knowledge in areas of *tafsīr*, *Ḥadīth*, etc. He should speak in a low voice, avoid quarrelling, and abstain from futile talks and arguments.

Thus, the person performing *iʿtikāf* should strive to benefit from his dwelling in the *masjid* to excel in worship and devotion, without involving himself in any of the worldly distractions.

Time of Year

Iʿtikāf may be performed at any time of the year. ʿĀʾishah (R) reported that the Prophet (ﷺ) performed *iʿtikāf* for ten days in *Shawwāl.* [3]

However, it is most recommended to perform *iʿtikāf* during *Ramaḍān*. This follows from the *ḥadīth* of Abū Hurayrah:

1 *Zād ul-Maʿād* (2:86-87).

2 *Laṭāʾif ul-Maʿārif* (p. 203).

3 Recorded by al-Bukhārī, Muslim, and Ibn Khuzaymah.

"Allāh's Messenger (ﷺ) used to perform *i'tikāf* for ten days during each *Ramaḍān*. On the year in which he passed, he performed *i'tikāf* for twenty days." [1]

The best days to perform *i'tikāf* are the last ten days of *Ramaḍān*, because these are the days on which *Laylat ul-Qadr* falls. 'Ā'ishah (R) reported:

"The Prophet (ﷺ) used to perform *i'tikāf* during the last ten days of *Ramaḍān* until Allāh (ﷻ) took his life." [2]

Place for *I'tikāf*

A Mosque of *Jumu'ah*

I'tikāf may only be performed in a *masjid*, as is indicated in the above *āyah* from *al-Baqarah* (2:187). Also, 'Ā'ishah (R) said:

"It is recommended for the one performing *i'tikāf* not to leave (the *masjid*) except for an essential need, not to visit a sick person, and not to touch or sleep with his wife. *I'tikāf* may only be performed in a *masjid* where the *jamā'ah* prayer is performed [or where *Jumu'ah* (Friday prayer) is offered]. And it is recommended for the one performing *i'tikāf* to fast." [3]

Thus, *i'tikāf* must be performed in a *masjid* where the *Jumu'ah* is held. This insures that one would not need to exit from it to attend the *Jumu'ah* prayer, which is an obligation on him.

---

1 Al-Bukhārī and Ibn Khuzaymah.

2 Al-Bukhārī, Muslim, and Ibn Khuzaymah.

3 Recorded by al-Bayhaqī with an authentic chain of narrators, and Abū Dāwūd with a good chain. The part between square brackets is from the latter.

THE THREE SACRED MOSQUES

A clear authentic *ḥadīth* further restricts the *masjid*s in the above *āyāh* (2:187) to only three: *al-Masjid ul-Ḥarām* (the Sacred Mosque of Makkah), *al-Masjid un-Nabawī* (the Prophet's Mosque at al-Madīnah), and *al-Masjid ul-Aqṣā* (the Furthest Mosque at Jerusalem).

A group of people performed *i'tikāf* in a *masjid* between the houses of 'Abdullāh Bin Mas'ūd and Abū Mūsā al-Ash'arī in al-Kūfah. So, Ḥuthayfah (ﷺ) asked Ibn Mas'ūd (ﷺ):

> "Do you hold the opinion that it is permissible to perform *i'tikāf* (at the *masjid*) between your house and Abū Mūsā's? You know that the Prophet (ﷺ) said:
>
> **‹*I'tikāf* should not to be performed except in the Three *Masjids*.›**"

Ibn Mas'ūd replied:

> "You may have forgotten (the meaning), and they (who are performing *i'tikāf* at the other *masjid*) remembered. Or you may be mistaken, and they be right!" [1]

Ibn Mas'ūd's response indicates that he does not deny the authenticity of this *ḥadīth*, but is only uncertain of its correct meaning. The truth in this case is to adhere to the apparent meaning of this *ḥadīth*.

A number of scholars among the *Salaf* have adhered to the text of this *ḥadīth*; among them are Ḥuthayfah Bin al-Yamān (ﷺ), Sa'īd Bin al-Musayyib, and 'Aṭā' (although 'Aṭā' did not mention *al-Aqṣā*). Others among the *Salaf* hold the opinion that *i'tikāf* may be performed at any *masjid* of *Jumu'ah*.

---

1 Recorded by aṭ-Ṭaḥāwī in *Mushkal ul-Āthār* (4:20), ath-Thahabī in *Siyaru A'lām in-Nubalā'* (15:81), al-Ismā'īlī, and al-Bayhaqī in *as-Sunan* (4:316), with an authentic chain from Ḥuthayfah Bin al-Yamān (ﷺ); it is proven authentic by ath-Thahabī and al-Albānī in *Silsilat ul-Aḥādīth iṣ-Ṣaḥīḥah* (No. 2786).

At Home?

Some scholars say that one may even perform *i'tikāf* at the part of one's home which is designated as prayer-place.

It is obvious that one should follow the opinion that agrees best with the authentic *ḥadīth*. And Allāh (ﷻ) knows best.

Requirements of *I'tikāf*

Staying Within the *Masjid*

As indicated above in the definition of *i'tikāf* as well as the *ḥadīth* of 'Ā'ishah (R), a *mu'takif* may not leave the boundaries of the *masjid*, except for a human need, such as eating or going to the toilet.

Fasting

It is commendable for the one performing *i'tikāf* to fast, as was stated earlier from 'Ā'ishah (R). Many scholars consider fasting a condition for *i'tikāf*, without which it is invalid. Ibn ul-Qayyim (r) said:

> "There is no report that the Prophet (ﷺ) performed *i'tikāf* without fasting; rather, 'Ā'ishah (R) said:
>
> '*I'tikāf* may not be performed without fasting.'
>
> Also, Allāh (ﷻ) only mentioned *i'tikāf* with fasting; and Allāh's Messenger (ﷺ) did not perform *i'tikāf* except while fasting. So the soundest opinion, which is held by the majority of the *Salaf*, is that: Fasting is a condition for *i'tikāf*. This is the opinion that *Shaykh ul-Islām* Abū al-'Abbās Ibn Taymiyyah favored." [1]

---

1 *Zād ul-Ma'ād.*

STARTING AND ENDING TIMES

It is recommended to start *iʿtikāf* in the morning, immediately after *fajr* prayer. ʿĀʾishah (R) reported:

> "When Allāh's Messenger (ﷺ) intended *iʿtikāf*, he would pray *fajr* then enter into his *iʿtikāf* place." [1]

It is recommended to end *iʿtikāf* in the morning as well. Al-Bukhārī headed one of the chapters in his *Ṣaḥīḥ* by the title, "Chapter concerning departing from *iʿtikāf* in the morning." He then cited the *ḥadīth* of Abū Saʿīd al-Khudrī (ﷺ):

> "We performed *iʿtikāf* with Allāh's Messenger (ﷺ) over the middle ten days (of *Ramaḍān*). On the morning of the twentieth, we moved our belongings." [2]

MINIMUM STAY

From the above, it is clear that one should stay for a minimum of one day and night in *iʿtikāf*. Thus, as declared by Ibn Taymiyyah [3], it is not permissible for one entering a *masjid* for prayer to intend to perform *iʿtikāf* during the time of his stay in it.

Permitted Acts During *Iʿtikāf*

LEAVING THE *MASJID* FOR A NEED

It is permissible for the one performing *iʿtikāf* to leave the *masjid* to fulfill a need, like going to the toilet or taking a required bath. One may also bring his head or a part of his body out of the *masjid*'s boundaries without invalidating his *iʿtikāf*. ʿĀʾishah (R) said:

---

1 Al-Bukhārī and Muslim.

2 Al-Bukhārī and Muslim.

3 In *al-Ikhtiyārāt*.

> "While Allāh's Messenger (ﷺ) was in the *Masjid* performing *i'tikāf*, he would bring his head (out of the *Masjid*) into my apartment (next to the *Masjid*), so that I would comb [and wash] his hair. Between us was only the threshold of the door, and I was menstruating. During his *i'tikāf*, he would not enter the house (completely) except for a human need." [1]

PERFORMING *WUḌŪ* WITHIN THE *MASJID*

It is permissible for one in *i'tikāf* to perform *wuḍū'* in the *masjid* [2]. A man who served the Prophet (ﷺ) said:

> "The Prophet (ﷺ) performed a light ablution in the *Masjid*." [3]

ERECTING A TENT INSIDE THE *MASJID*

It is permissible for one in *i'tikāf* to pitch a small tent in the rear of the *masjid* to retire to and perform his worship in seclusion [4]. Allāh's Messenger (ﷺ) requested 'Ā'ishah (R) to erect a skin tent for him while he was in *i'tikāf* [5]. He (ﷺ) also performed *i'tikāf* under a small canopy with a straw mat covering its door. [6]

---

1 Al-Bukhārī, Muslim, Ibn Abū Shaybah, and Aḥmad.

2 Note that this is not possible in most of the contemporary *masjid*s, because they are tiles or carpeted, contrary to the Prophet's (ﷺ) *Masjid* whose floor was stone and earth.

3 Recorded by al-Bayhaqī with a good *isnād*, and by Aḥmad with an authentic *isnād*.

4 As in the above note, this is also not possible in most of today's *masjid*s, because of the way they are structured. However, one may reserve for himself a specific corner of the mosque where he spends most of his time during *i'tikāf*.

5 Al-Bukhārī and Muslim.

6 Muslim and Ibn Khuzaymah.

Using a Mattress

A *mu'takif* may lay down a mattress or mat in a corner of the *masjid* for his sleep. Ibn 'Umar (رضي الله عنه) reported that when Allāh's Messenger (ﷺ) performed *i'tikāf*, a mattress or bed would be laid down for him behind the pillar of at-Tawbah. [1]

Disapproved Acts During *I'tikāf*

Leaving Without Need

As indicated above, leaving the *masjid* without need contradicts the basic definition of *i'tikāf*, and the way the Prophet (ﷺ) performed it. It therefore invalidates it; Ibn Ḥazm said:

> "The scholars agree that any *mu'takif* who departs from the *masjid* without a need, necessity, or obligatory act of righteousness, then his *i'tikāf* is invalidated." [2]

Intercourse

I'tikāf is nullified by intercourse, as Allāh (ﷻ) said:

﴿وَلَا تُبَٰشِرُوهُنَّ وَأَنتُمْ عَٰكِفُونَ فِى ٱلْمَسَٰجِدِ﴾ البقرة ١٨٧

«**And have no contact with them while performing** *i'tikāf* **in the** *masjids*.» [3]

Ibn 'Abbās (رضي الله عنه) said:

> "If a *mu'takif* performs intercourse, he invalidates his

---

1 Recorded by Ibn Mājah and al-Bayhaqī. Its *isnād* is *ḥasan* (*Sifatu Ṣawm in-Nabī*).
2 *Marātib ul-Ijmā'* (p.48).
3 *Al-Baqarah* 2:187.

i'tikāf, and would have to start over." [1]

Yet there is no authentic text requiring a specific *kaffārah* (expiation) for the person who invalidates his *i'tikāf* like that.

WORLDLY INVOLVEMENT

Getting involved in worldly matters contradicts the spirit and meaning of *i'tikāf*, where one is supposed to retreat in seclusion for the mere purpose of worshipping Allāh (ﷻ) without distractions.

A *mu'takif* who wastes his time in futile talks and arguments, revilement and cursing, or other similar acts, reduces and spoils the reward and value of his *i'tikāf*. Ibn ul-Qayyim says:

> "The goal of this (good conduct) is to fulfill the purpose and spirit of *i'tikāf*. This is contrary to the practice of those ignorant ones, who make their place of *i'tikāf* a meeting place for visiting, chatting, and gossip. This is indeed contrary to the Prophetic *i'tikāf*!" [2]

Women's *I'tikāf*

It is permissible for a woman to visit her husband while he is performing *i'tikāf*, and for him to walk with her to the *masjid*'s door. Ṣafiyyah (R) said:

> "The Prophet (ﷺ) was performing *i'tikāf* in the *Masjid* during the last ten days of *Ramaḍān*. I went to visit him one night. Some of his wives were with him, and left soon after. I talked with him for a while, then stood up to return home; he said, **‹Wait, let me escort you.›** And he walked with me (toward my dwelling in the house of Usāmah Bin Zayd). When we reached the door of the

1 Ibn Abī Shaybah and 'Abd ur-Razzāq with an authentic chain of narrators.

2 *Zād ul-Ma'ād*.

> *Masjid* closest to the door of Umm Salamah's house, two men from the *Anṣār* passed by; when they saw the Prophet (ﷺ) they hurried; and he (ﷺ) called out to them, **‹Slow down! This is my wife Ṣafiyyah Bint Ḥuyayy.›** They said, "*Subḥānallāh* (exalted is Allāh)! O Messenger of Allāh [1]!" So he (ﷺ) said:
>
> **‹Satan flows in the human being the way blood flows in veins. I feared that he may have suggested some evil to your hearts.›**" [2]

It is even permissible for a woman to perform *iʿtikāf* with her husband, or by herself. ʿĀ'ishah (R) said:

> "One of the wives of Allāh's Messenger [in one narration: Umm Salamah] performed *iʿtikāf* with him while she had post menstrual bleeding in which she saw red or yellowish traces; and sometimes we put a tray beneath her while she prayed." [3]

She also said:

> "The Prophet (ﷺ) performed *iʿtikāf* for the last ten days of *Ramaḍān* until Allāh took him; then his wives performed the *iʿtikāf* after him." [4]

This establishes that women are allowed to perform *iʿtikāf*. However, this has two conditions:

1. Prior permission from the woman's *walī* (guardian).

---

1 They expressed surprise that the Prophet (ﷺ) would expect them to entertain any suspicious thoughts about him.

2 Al-Bukhārī, Muslim, Abū Dāwūd.

3 Recorded by al-Bukhārī and Saʿīd Bin Manṣūr.

4 Al-Bukhārī, Muslim and others.

2. Confidence that the presence of the woman performing *i'tikāf* in the *masjid* would not cause *fitnah* (temptation) or *khulwah* (seclusion) with men.

If either of these two requirements cannot be fulfilled, *i'tikāf* is not permitted for a woman, as the *fiqh* principle indicates:

> "Warding off evil is more important than establishing good."

CHAPTER 9

PERFECTING THE PRAYER

Devotion in the Prayer

Reports from the Prophet and the *Salaf*

A Muslim should always strive to be a good example of a righteous believer: obedient to his Lord, and adhering to His Prophet's *Sunnah*. This is a general rule, which should be applied to the *qiyām* prayer as well. In this regard, the Prophet (ﷺ) said:

> **‹Whoever stands in prayer during *Ramaḍān* out of faith and expectation (of Allāh's reward), all of his previous sins will be forgiven.›** [1]

Earlier in this book, we have discussed many details concerning the Prophet's (ﷺ) *qiyām* during *Ramaḍān*, as well as other times. We described how his prayer was extremely long and devoted, as in 'Ā'ishah's report:

> "... He would pray four *rak'āt*, and do not ask how good and long they were ..."

And her report:

> "He would stay in *sujūd* as long as one of you would read fifty *āyāt*."

And Ḥuthayfah's report:

> "... Then he read *al-Baqarah* (in the first *rak'ah*); then

---

1 Recorded by al-Bukhārī, Muslim and others.

> he made *rukūʿ*; and his *rukūʿ* was comparable (in duration) to his standing ..."

Ḥu<u>th</u>ayfah then described the Prophet's long standing after *rukūʿ* and his long *sujūd* after that.

Furthermore, the *Salaf* during the time of ʿUmar (ﷺ) recited long portions of *Qurʾān* in *tarāwīḥ*. When ʿUmar summoned the reciters and commanded them to lead the people in *tarāwīḥ*, "He (ﷺ) instructed the fast reciters to recite thirty *āyāt*, the intermediate to recite twenty five, and the slow to recite twenty." [1]

Thus they would recite about three hundred *āyāt* – until some people behind them had to lean on canes because of the long duration of the prayer. And they did not finish their prayer until close to *fajr* time.

In addition, they would make the various parts of prayer comparable in length to the recitation. They would make long *rukūʿ* and *sujūd*, uttering during them numerous forms of *<u>th</u>ikr* and supplications, in accordance with the *Sunnah* [2].

This should motivate us to imitate them in our prayer as much as possible, making it long, and saying plenty of *tasbīḥ* (*'subḥān Allāh* – exalted is Allāh) and *<u>th</u>ikr* during *rukūʿ*, *sujūd*, and in between. With that, we hope to attain, at least, some level of *khushūʿ* (devotion), which is the spirit and core of the prayer.

Lost Devotion

The majority of Muslims have given up *khushūʿ* in the *qiyām* prayers, in exchange for their insistence on praying twenty *rakʿāt*, which they wrongly attribute to ʿUmar (ﷺ). They are more concerned about maintaining this number than about having *khushūʿ* and tranquility in the prayer!

We see many *imāms* shorten the recitation in *tarāwīḥ* to such a degree that they barely read anything after *al-Fātiḥah*. And even for *al-Fātiḥah*, they read it so fast, that they have completely lost its beauty

---

1 Recorded by Ibn Abī Shaybah (2:89:2) and al-Faryābī (2:76) with an authentic *isnād*.

2 For details concerning this, review *Ṣifatu Ṣalāt in-Nabī* by al-Albānī.

and sweetness. In their quest for speed, they also recite it with one breath, contrary to what is confirmed from the Prophet (ﷺ) that he used to read it one *āyah* by one *āyah*.

And if you find among those *imāms* some who recite longer, they still neglect the *sunnah* of making the various parts of prayer comparable to the recitation in length, as in Ḥuthayfah's *ḥadīth* above. They all pray like pecking roosters, or gears and machines going up and down in a mechanical way, unable to comprehend or contemplate what they hear of Allāh's (ﷻ) words. It's even hard for one to keep up with them without extreme difficulty!

Many authors dealing with the subject of *tarāwīḥ* do not even try to draw the Muslims' attention to the importance of *khushūʿ*, as if it is not a relevant matter. They persistently direct their efforts to establishing twenty *rakʿāt*, regardless of how they are performed, and how close they are to the Prophet's prayer.

Glimpses of Light

We do not want to neglect, however, the increasing number of authors and *imāms* who have realized the appalling manner in which *tarāwīḥ* is commonly performed, thereby reverting to praying eleven *rakʿāt* with tranquility and *khushūʿ* – may Allāh (ﷻ) increase their numbers, and keep them firm in guidance, adherence to the *Sunnah*, and perseverance in reviving it.

Ḥadīths on Perfecting the Prayer

In what follows, we cite a number of authentic *ḥadīths* calling on Muslims to perform the prayers in a good way, and warning them from neglecting that. By this, we hope to remind the readers of the importance of perfecting all of their prayers – *farḍ* and *nafl*, *qiyām* or otherwise.

1. Abū Hurayrah (ﷺ) reported:

"A man entered the *Masjid* and prayed while Allāh's

Messenger (ﷺ) was sitting in a corner of the *Masjid*. After finishing, the man went to the Messenger (ﷺ) and said the *Salām* (peace be on you) to him. He (ﷺ) replied, **‹*Wa ʿalayk as-Salām* (and upon you be peace); go back and pray, because you have not prayed!›** So he went back, prayed, and then came back and said the *Salām* again to the Prophet (ﷺ). He (ﷺ) replied, **‹*Wa ʿalayk as-Salām*; go back and pray, because you have not prayed. ›** (This repeated three times). After the third time, the man said, "I do not know how to pray better, so teach me, O Messenger of Allāh." He (ﷺ) said:

‹When you intend to pray,
perform *wuḍū'* in a complete manner;
then face the *Qiblah* (direction of Makkah), say '*Allāhu Akbar* (Allāh is the Greatest),' and recite as much of *Qur'ān* as is convenient for you;
then bow down until you achieve tranquility in bowing;
then raise you head until you stand level;
then prostrate yourself until you achieve tranquility in prostration;
then sit up until you are level in sitting;
then prostrate yourself until you achieve tranquility in prostration;
then stand up until you are level in your standing;
then do the same in the rest of your prayer.›" [1]

2. Abū Masʿūd al-Badrī (رضي الله عنه) reported that Allāh's Messenger (ﷺ) said:

‹One's prayer is not acceptable unless he makes his back straight during bowing and prostration.› [2]

---

1 Recorded by al-Bukhārī, Muslim, and others.

2 Recorded by Abū Dāwūd, an-Nasā'ī, at-Tirmiḏhī, Ibn Mājah, ad-Dārimī, aṭ-Ṭaḥāwī

3. Abū Hurayrah (ﷺ) reported that Allāh's Messenger (ﷺ) said:

> **‹The worst thief among people is he who steals from his prayer.›**

He was asked, "How would one steal from his prayer, O Messenger of Allāh?" He replied, **‹By not completing the *rukū'* and *sujūd*.›** [1]

4. The Muslim army generals, 'Amr Bin al-'Āṣ, Khālid Bin al-Walīd, Sharḥabīl Bin Ḥasanah, and Yazīd Bin Abī Sufyān (ﷺ), all reported that Allāh's Messenger (ﷺ) saw a man not completing his *rukū'*, and pecking in his *sujūd* during the prayer. He (ﷺ) said:

> **‹If this man dies upon his current state, he would die upon a religion other than that of Muḥammad – pecking in his prayer like a crow pecking blood! The example of one who does not complete *rukū'* and pecks in his *sujūd* is like that of a hungry person who eats one or two dates that do not satisfy his hunger in the least bit.›** [2]

5. Ṭalq Bin 'Alī (ﷺ) reported that Allāh's Messenger (ﷺ):

(*al-Mushkal* 1:80), aṭ-Ṭayālisī, Aḥmad, and ad-Dāraquṭnī who said, 'It's *isnād* is confirmed and authentic.' It is indeed as he said, because al-A'mash (one of the narrators) declared hearing (from the narrator above him)), as in the report of aṭ-Ṭayālisī.

1 Recorded by al-Ḥākim who considered it authentic; and ath-Thahabī agreed with him. It has a witness recorded by al-Ḥākim from Abū Qatādah (ﷺ), and another witness recorded by Mālik from an-Nu'mān Bin Murrah, whose *isnād* is authentic, though *mursal*; it also has a third witness recorded by aṭ-Ṭayālisī from Abū Sa'īd al-Khudrī (ﷺ), which was verified to be authentic by as-Suyūṭī in *Tanwīr ul-Ḥawālik*.

2 Recorded by al-Ājirī (in *al-Arba'īn*) and al-Bayhaqī. Its *isnād* is *ḥasan*. Also, al-Munthirī said, "Recorded by aṭ-Ṭabarānī (in *al-Kabīr*) and Abū Ya'lā with a *ḥasan isnād*, as well as Ibn Khuzaymah in his *Ṣaḥīḥ*."

‹Verily, Allāh (ﷻ) does not look at the prayer of the person who does not straighten his spine between *rukū*ʿ and *sujūd*.› [1]

6. ʿAmmār Bin Yāsir (ؓ) said that he heard Allāh's Messenger (ﷺ) say:

‹A person would pray a prayer, and nothing recorded for him (of its reward) except one-tenth of it, one-ninth, one-eighth, one-seventh, one-sixth, one-fifth, one-quarter one-third, or one-half.› [2]

This *ḥadīth* means that, "Peoples' rewards vary in accordance with their *khushū*ʿ, devotion, and other manners that conform with perfecting the prayer." [3]

7. ʿAbdullāh Bin ash-Shikhkhīr (ؓ) said:

"I came to the Prophet (ﷺ) while he was praying, and his chest was making a whirring sound like that of a boiling pot (from crying)." [4]

---

1 Recorded by Aḥmad, aṭ-Ṭabarānī (in *al-Kabīr*), and aḍ-Ḍiyāʾ ul-Maqdisī (in *al-Mukhtārah*); its *isnād* is authentic. It also has a witness in *al-Musnad* with acceptable narrators, which was judged authentic by al-Ḥāfiẓ al-ʿIrāqī in *Takhrīj ul-Iḥyāʾ*, and al-Munthirī said that its *isnād* is good.

2 Recorded by Abū Dāwūd, al-Bayhaqī, and Aḥmad with two different chains, of which one was judged to be authentic by al-Ḥāfiẓ al-ʿIrāqī. It is also recorded by Ibn Ḥibbān in his *Ṣaḥīḥ*, as was stated in *at-Targhīb*.

3 *Fayḍ ul-Qadīr* by al-Manāwī.

4 Recorded by Abū Dāwūd, al-Nasāʾī, al-Bayhaqī, and Aḥmad, with an authentic *isnād* that conforms with the condition of Muslim. It is also recorded by Ibn Khuzaymah and Ibn Ḥibbān in their *Ṣaḥīḥs*, as is mentioned in *at-Targhīb*.

Conclusion

These noble *ḥadīth*s apply generally to all prayers, whether *farḍ* or *nafl*, and whether they are day or night prayers. The scholars have noted this in regard to the *tarāwīḥ* prayer in particular; so an-Nawawī said:

> "The very manner of performing *tarāwīḥ* is similar to what was explained earlier for other prayers; all the preceding *thikr*s apply to it, such as the opening supplication and others, completion of *tashahhud* and the supplication that follows it, and other things that were previously mentioned. Even though this appears to be obvious and well known, I note it here because many people neglect it and omit most of the *thikr*s during *tarāwīḥ*. And the truth is what is mentioned here." [1]

Al-ʿĀmirī said:

> "A matter of great concern that requires noting is that the multitudes of *imām*s who lead people in *tarāwīḥ* have gotten into the practice of shortening the reading, abbreviating the various parts, and omitting *thikr*s. The scholars have said, 'The method of performing it is similar to that of other prayers in terms of conditions, various manners, and all *thikr*s, such as the opening supplication, *thikr*s during the various parts, the supplication after *tashahhud*, etc.'
>
> Some of those *imām*s also try to read the *āyāt* mentioning Allāh's mercy, timing their recitation so as to make *rukūʿ* only when they reach them; by doing this they neglect two important etiquettes for recitation during the prayer: they sometimes make the second *rakʿah* longer than the first; and they pause between *āyāt* that are linked in meaning.

---

1 *Al-Athkār*; chapter on "The *athkār* of the *tarāwīḥ* Prayer'.

The reason for all this is that the *sunnah*s have been neglected, becoming largely obliterated, to the extent that the one who adheres to them is now considered ignorant by many people because he differs with the majority; this is caused by the spread of evil in our time, as the Prophet (ﷺ) said:

‹The hour will not arrive until (prior to that) the right becomes wrong, and the wrong right.› [1]

Thus be sure to adhere to the *Sunnah*: require it from yourself, and command those who obey you with it. By this you will be saved, secure and happy. The honorable al-Fuḍayl Bin ʿAyyāḍ (r) said, 'Do not feel lonely on the road of guidance because of the scarcity of its travellers; and do not be awed by the doomed hordes.' " [2]

1 This meaning appears in many *ḥadīth*s, recorded by aṭ-Ṭabarānī in *al-Awṣaṭ*, Abū Nuʿaym in *al-Ḥulyah*, Ibn Waḍḍāḥ, Ibn Mājah, and others. Some of the reports have been judged to be authentic by al-ʿAsqalānī, al-Haythamī, and others.

2 Near the end of al-ʿAmirī's book, "*Bahjat ul-Maḥāfil wa-Bughyat ul-Amāthil fī Talkhīṣ is-Siyari wal-muʿjizāti wash-shamāʾil*".

CHAPTER 10

SUMMARY

Discussions in this book have extended beyond our initial expectations. This is something unavoidable, because it is demanded by any correct scholarly study. Because of this, we decided to present our worthy readers with a summary in this chapter, which will make it easier for quick reference and application – *in shāʾa ʿLlāh.*

Important Points

1. Praying *Tarāwīḥ* in *Jamāʿah* Is a *Sunnah*

Praying *tarāwīḥ* in *jamāʿah* is a *sunnah* and not *bidʿah.* The Prophet (ﷺ) prayed it in *jamāʿah* on many nights; and the reason for stopping was only his fear that some people among his *Ummah* would think that it is obligatory if he were consistent in it. This fear ended with the completion of the *Sharīʿah* (the *Islām*ic Law) when he (ﷺ) passed away.

2. The Correct Number in the *Sunnah* Is Eleven

The Prophet (ﷺ) prayed eleven *rakʿāt* for *tarāwīḥ*. The *ḥadīth* claiming that he prayed twenty *rakʿāt* is very weak.

It is not permissible to pray more than eleven *rakʿāt*, because that conflicts with his practice and his command, **‹Pray as you have seen me pray.›** Because of this, it's not permissible to add to the *sunnah* of *fajr* or others.

3. Our View of Those Who Disagree

For those who pray more than eleven for *tarāwīḥ*, we neither consider them innovators nor misguided – if their position results from the

Sunnah not being apparent to them, and not because they follow their desires.

4. The *Sunnah* Is Better than the Addition

Even if one concedes that it is permissible to add to the number of *tarāwīḥ,* there is no doubt that it is best to adhere to the number that the Prophet (ﷺ) prayed, because he said, **‹The best guidance is that of Muḥammad.›**

5. ʿUmar Revived the *Sunnah*

ʿUmar (ؓ) did not innovate in the *tarāwīḥ* prayer; rather, he revived the *sunnah* of praying it in *jamāʿah*; and he maintained the number of its *rakʿāt* in accordance to the *Sunnah.* Whatever was reported differently from him is not authentic in any of its chains; and those chains are such that they do not reinforce each other.

6. The *Ṣaḥābah* Did Not Pray Twenty

It is not confirmed that any of the *ṣaḥābah* prayed twenty *rakʿāt* for *tarāwīḥ.* Therefore, one must adhere to the number of *rakʿāt* established in the *Sunnah* and confirmed by ʿUmar (ؓ). The Prophet (ﷺ) has commanded us to follow his *Sunnah* and the *sunnah* of the Rightly Guided *Khulafāʾ*.

7. No Excuse for Adding

Even if we assume that adding to the correct number of *rakʿāt* was authentically reported from some of the *ṣaḥābah* (which is not the case), we would have to consider that it was for a specific excuse that does not hold today.

8. Scholars Disapproving the Addition

Praying more than eleven was disapproved by Mālik, Ibn al-ʿArabī, and many other scholars. Furthermore, there is absolutely no *ijmāʿ*

(consensus) for twenty *rakʿāt* among the *ṣaḥābah* or the great scholars.

9. Position from the Great Scholars

Rejecting additional *rakʿāt* does not imply rejecting the notable scholars who have allowed them. Disagreeing with them in this issue does not, by any means, imply belittling their knowledge and understanding.

10. Lost Devotion

Insisting on adding to the reported number has caused people to pray in a hasty manner, losing *khushūʿ* and, very often, correctness of the prayer.

11. Praying less than Eleven

Even though it is not permissible to pray more than eleven *rakʿāt*, it is permissible to pray less, down to as few as only one *rakʿah*. This is established in the *Sunnah* and the practice of the *Salaf*.

12. Various Methods for Praying *Qiyām*

The different manners in which the Prophet (ﷺ) prayed *qiyām* and *witr* are all permissible. The best manner is to pray eleven *rakʿāt* with long recitation, making *taslīm* at the end of every pair of *rakʿāt*.

Lastly

The following are the words with which al-Albānī concluded his book *Ṣalāt ut-Tarāwīḥ*:

> "This is the end of what Allāh (ﷻ) has facilitated for me compiling on the subject of the *tarāwīḥ* prayer. If I was right, it is by the blessing of Allāh (ﷻ), to whom belongs all glory and bounties. And if it is the other

possibility, then I implore everyone who finds a mistake to point it to me; and Allāh (ﷻ) will reward him.

Exalted are You, O Allāh; all praise belongs to You; I testify that there is no true god except You; I seek Your forgiveness; and I repent to You.

May Allāh bestow his *ṣalāh* and peace upon the Illiterate Prophet, and all of his family and companions. And the last of our calls is, *al-ḥamdu li 'Llāhi rabb il-'ālamīn.*"

INDEX OF ARABIC TERMS

Al-Anṣār	*111*
Al-Fātiḥah	*94*
Al-Lawḥ ul-Maḥfūẓ	*22*
Al-Masjid ul-Aqṣā	*130*
Al-Masjid ul-Ḥarām	*126*
Al-Masjid un-Nabawī	*130*
Athān	*96*
Āyah	*xxiii*
Āyāt	*xxiii*
Bid'ah	*xiv*
Da'wah	*xiv*
Dīn	*xvi*
Du'ā'	*xxiv*
Fajr	*32*
Falāḥ	*30*
Fatwā	*44*
Fiqh	
Fuqahā'	*1*
Fitnah	*1, 137*
Ghayb	*1*
Ḥadīth	*xix*
Ḥāfiẓ	*45, 51*
Hajada	*7*
Tahajjud	*7*
Ḥajj	*126*
Ḥasan	*1*
Hawā	*5*
Ḥukm	*80*
Ḥākim	*80*
Ijmā'	*65*
Imām	*8*
Iqāmah	*97*
Istisqā'	*70*
I'ḍāl	*61*
Jahl	*126*
Jāhiliyyah	*126*
Jamā'ah	*29*
Jāmi'	*129*
Jannah	*9*
Jihād	
Mujāhid	*109*
Juhd	*80*
Ijtihād	*80*
Jumu'ah	*129*
Kafara	
Kāfir	*121*
Kuffār	*120*
Kufr	*72*
Kaffārah	*135*
Khalafa	
Khalīfah	*15*
Khilāfah	*15*
Khulafā'	*2*
Khulwah	*137*
Khushū'	*140*
Khutbat ul-Ḥājah	*32*
Kusūf	*70*
Maghrib	*101*
Marfū'	*1*
Masjid	*xxv*
Mathhab	*xvii, 65*
Mawqūf	*1, 59*
Munkar	*47, 52*
Munqati'	*55*
Mursal	*29, 55*
Mu'awwithāt	*101*

Nafl 7
Qadar 21
Qadr 21
  Laylat ul-Qadr 21
Qanata 109
  Qānit 109
  Qunūt 82, 109
Qaṣr 69
Qiblah 142
Qiyām 7
  Qiyām ul-Layl 7
Raka'a 2
  Rak'ah 2
  Rak'āt 2
  Rukū' 2
Sabaḥa
  Subḥān Allāh 140
  Tasbīḥ 140
Ṣaḥābah xv
  Ṣaḥābī xv
Ṣaḥīḥ 1
Saḥūr 30
Sajada 24
  Masjid 24
  Sujūd 24
Salaf xv
Ṣalāh xxiii
  Ṣalāt ul-Layl 7
Salām 142
  Taslīm 94
Sanada
  Isnād 92
  Sanad 16
Shaf' 101
Shahādah 32
  Tashahhud 32
Shar' 7
  Sharī'ah 147
  Shar'ī 39
Shāth 53
Shaykh 59
Shirk xvii
  Mushrik xix
Shuhadā' 16
Siddīqīn 15
Siwāk 95
  Miswāk 16
  Tasawwuk 16
Sunnah xiv
Sūrah xxiii
Tābi'ī 29
  Tābi'īn 29
  Tābi'ūn 29
Tafsīr xxiii
Takbīr 122
Taqlīd 2
Tarāwīḥ 7
Tarbiyah xv
Taṣfiyah xv
Taslīm 96
Thikr xxiv, 2
Uḍḥiyah 61
Umm ul-Qur'ān 94
Ummah 39
Walī 136
Witr 7, 92
Wuḍū' 10
Zakāh 15
Ẓuhr 71
'Abd xiii
'Akafa 125
  I'tikāf 125
  Ma'kūf 125
  Mu'takif 125

AL-QUR'ĀN WAS-SUNNAH SOCIETY
OF NORTH AMERICA

Al-Qur'ān was-Sunnah Society is distinguished by its clear and firm *manhaj* (methodology), the *manhaj* of the righteous *Salaf*: the Companions (ﷺ) of the Prophet (ﷺ) and their true followers. This *manhaj* centers around:

a) *Tawḥīd*,
b) adherence to the *Qur'ān* and *Sunnah*, and
c) following the guidance of the *Salaf*.

The goal of the Society is to guide people to *Islām*, and help them understand it, practice it, and call to it, in accordance with this blessed *Manhaj*.

In order to fulfill this, the Society attempts to (a) cooperate with Muslim individuals and organizations, and (b) present *Islām*, pure and clear, to the non-Muslims, and invite them to it.

Al-Qur'ān was-Sunnah Society emphasizes mature work, abandoning *'aṣabiyyah* (factionism), and honoring the *'ulamā'* (learned scholars of *Islām*).

We ask Allāh (ﷻ) to grant us truthfulness, sincerity, and perseverance in obeying Him. If this be granted, then we are certain of His help and support; indeed, there is no true help and support except from Him.

P.O. Box 19900, Cincinnati, OH 45219, USA • ✆ 606-578-8371 • FAX: 606-578-8372